S. SEKOU ABODUNRIN

Cherish
the Local Church

Understanding His thrill in our assembling

Cherish the local Church

Understanding His thrill in our assembling

Sekou Publishing

sekou@sekou.me

Copyright © 2020 by Sekou Abodunrin

Cover Design and Page Layout
Kenteba Kreations
contact.kenteba@gmail.com

ISBN: 978-1-912921-04-1
Published by Sekou Publishing. All rights reserved.

Unless otherwise indicated, all Scripture quotations are taken from the King James Version of the Bible.

Some Scripture quotations marked (AMP) are taken from The Amplified Bible (AMP) Copyright © 2015 by The Lockman Foundation, La Habra, CA 90631. All rights reserved.

Some Scripture quotations marked (NASB) are taken from The New American Standard Bible 1995 (NASB) New American Standard Bible®, Copyright © 1960, 1971, 1977, 1995 by The Lockman Foundation. All rights reserved.;

Some Scripture quotations marked (NET) are taken from The New English Translation (NET) NET Bible® copyright ©1996-2017 by Biblical Studies Press, L.L.C. http://netbible.com All rights reserved.

Some Scripture quotations marked (NIV) are taken from THE HOLY BIBLE, NEW INTERNATIONAL VERSION®. Copyright© 1973, 1978, 1984, 2011 by Biblica, Inc.™. Used by permission of Zondervan

Some Scripture quotations marked (NLT) are taken from The New Living Translation (NLT) Holy Bible, New Living Translation, copyright © 1996, 2004,

Table of Contents

Introduction

The Lord Jesus teaches that the way we understand God's word is the way we worship God. It is impossible to correctly worship God apart from the right division of the written word. To achieve this, God uses men to teach us His word together with other saints. To grow spiritually, you'll need to be deliberate with the men that you associate with. The Christian walk is a walk with God, who brings us into contact with other saints, for God uses His men to influence other men. There is no real meaningful Christian growth away from other members of the family.

The man or woman that receives the gospel has received an eternal relationship with Christ and His brethren, which changes how the saints face every other relationship. The indwelling Spirit of God will cause the saint to crave community.

Although it is the manner of some to forsake assembly with other saints, as we comb through the scriptures, we find that there is no scriptural training to stay away from the assembling of ourselves together. Our assembling is how we experience God's gift of family. We fulfil God's plan by exhorting and encouraging each other in God's love to stir each other in the service of God. Therefore, there are no effective disciples of Christ who are effective all by themselves.

Paul made this thought-provoking statement regarding ministry in Troas "Furthermore, when I came to Troas to preach Christ's gospel, and a door was opened unto me of the Lord, I had no rest in my spirit, because I found not Titus my brother: but taking my leave of them, I went from thence into Macedonia" (see 2 Corinthians 2:12,13).

Paul admitted that although the Lord had opened a door for him in

Troas, he had no rest in his spirit because he could not find Titus. Such was the importance of the face-to-face fellowship that Titus supplied, that Paul did not take that open door!

This is quite a submission from a man that had hazarded his life for the gospel throughout his ministerial life. Although he was frequently in prisons, beaten severally with rods, stoned, in hunger and thirst, and shipwrecked for the gospel's sake, but despite all this, he pressed on. Interestingly, he always got back on his feet to take the gospel into new territories. None of his many travails caused him to draw back when the opportunity to preach the word presented itself.

Yet, when he could not find "Titus my brother", he took his leave of ministry in Troas.

The saint is not designed to be spiritually effective without the fellowship of other saints.

Paul's ministry could be condensed into two words – local churches. He was either filling new converts with them to form new ones, visiting them, praying for them, or writing to them. The local church must be emphasized. We must understand what it is and why it is so important. It is how we gift others with our presence, service, and fellowship.

We are to find out God's plan for the local church. We must never allow modernization, the pressure of social media, and the fear of men to silence us, otherwise, the truth of the local church will be hidden from the precious saints who so desperately need to know that the Lord has prepared a place where things can be done decently and in order.

This is written in the hope that we might have those local assemblies where we form and deepen our conviction and practice concerning the ways of the Lord concerning His church, its structure, its men, and its operation.

Kent, 2020

Acknowledgement

This book is dedicated to the precious saints at GracePlace with whom I have patiently sought to understand and practice the reality of the local church. Together, we continue to prioritise the nationality, tribe, and custom of the word above whatever tribe and culture we had before encountering God's word rightly divided.

I am indebted to many excellent teachers of the generations gone before, whose diligence in the Word has stimulated my thinking and caused me to see the place of strong local churches in redemption.
To Olatundun for patiently bearing with my musing over many of the things in this book through the years and for daring to believe when she could so easily not have. For our long and intense conversations on the right practice of the local church. Let's continue those conversations.

I will build my church

45. Philip findeth Nathanael, and saith unto him, We have found him, of whom Moses in the law, and the prophets, did write, Jesus of Nazareth, the son of Joseph.
John 1:45

Phillip, a student of John the Baptist, concluded that John's message meant that Jesus was the object of the ministries of Moses and the prophets.

What was John's message?

This was John's message:

29. The next day John seeth Jesus coming unto him, and saith, Behold the Lamb of God, which taketh away the sin of the world. 35. Again the next day after John stood, and two of his disciples; 36. And looking upon Jesus as he walked, he saith, Behold the Lamb of God!
John 1:29,35-36

As John taught his disciples the scriptures, he pointed out Jesus to them as "the Lamb of God". By referring to Jesus as "Lamb of God," John wants them to see Jesus as the fulfilment of all the rituals in their Jerusalem temple.

40. One of the two which heard John speak, and followed him, was Andrew, Simon Peter's brother. 41. He first findeth his own brother Simon, and saith unto him, We have found the Messias, which is, being interpreted, the Christ. 42. And he brought him to Jesus. And when Jesus beheld him, he said, Thou art Simon the son of Jona: thou shalt be called Cephas, which is by interpretation, A stone.
John 1:40-42

Andrew, one of John's disciples, repeated his teaching "we have found the Messias" to Peter.

Likewise, Phillip, having been exposed to John's ministry, told Nathaniel of John's teaching concerning Jesus.

45. Then Philip went to look for his friend, Nathanael, and told him, "We've found him! We've found the One we've been waiting for! It's Jesus, son of Joseph from Nazareth, the Anointed One! He's the One that Moses and the prophets prophesied would come!".
John 1:45 (TPT)

Phillip's words were, "He's the One that Moses and the prophets prophesied would come!"

Thus, in Phillip's testimony, we see that John had been teaching from the writings of Moses in the law, as well as the writings of the prophets. John's teaching ministry was from the scriptures. Andrew, Peter, Nathaniel and Phillip, as well as many others who had listened to John, had heard John clearly teach about Jesus' true identity from the scriptures.

Did the people accept John's testimony?

13. When Jesus came into the coasts of Caesarea Philippi, he asked his disciples, saying, Whom do men say that I the Son of man am? 14. And they said, Some say that thou art John the Baptist: some, Elias; and others, Jeremias, or one of the prophets.
Matthew 16:13-14

We can grasp that the people had heard John's teaching about Jesus from the law of Moses and the prophets. However, it appears they had not listened well because rather than admit that He was the Christ of scripture, they confused Jesus with one of the prophets that had spoken about Him.

Although John had correctly taught the testimony of the prophets, the people's unbelief concerning John's testimony indicated their unbelief towards the testimony in the Law of Moses and the writings of the prophets.

Moses and the prophets spoke concerning Christ:

> *25. Then he said unto them, O fools, and slow of heart to believe all that the prophets have spoken: 26. Ought not Christ to have suffered these things, and to enter into his glory? 27. And beginning at Moses and all the prophets, he expounded unto them in all the scriptures the things concerning himself.*
> *Luke 24:25-27*

Therefore, Jesus showed that the writings of Moses and all the prophets were concerning His sufferings and His glory (resurrection):

> *44. And he said unto them, These are the words which I spake unto you, while I was yet with you, that all things must be fulfilled, which were written in the law of Moses, and in the prophets, and in the psalms, concerning me. 45. Then opened he their understanding, that they might understand the scriptures,*
> *Luke 24:44-45*

Jesus used the fact of Christ as the common thread in the law of Moses, the prophets, and the psalms to open the understanding of His disciples so they could understand the scriptures.

> *39. "You are busy analyzing the Scriptures, frantically poring over them in hopes of gaining eternal life. Everything you read points to me,*
> *John 5:39 (TPT)*

Jesus explained that the scriptures are the story of Christ, for they testify of Him.

46. For had ye believed Moses, ye would have believed me: for he wrote of me.
John 5:46

Jesus showed that the person who accepts Moses' testimony would believe Jesus. A person who rejects Jesus only does so because they did not believe Moses.

Now back to the people's answer to Jesus' question:

14. And they said, Some say that thou art John the Baptist: some, Elias; and others, Jeremias, or one of the prophets.
Matthew 16:14

Therefore, if the people had paid attention to the law of Moses, the Prophets, and the Psalms and taken time to understand those prophecies and writings as taught by John, they would have correctly recognised Jesus.

Jesus' question, "whom do men say that I the Son of man am?" is really a question gauging their understanding of the holy scriptures. In their answer, we'll know whether the people believed John, the law of Moses, the prophets, and the psalms.

15. He saith unto them, But whom say ye that I am?
Matthew 13:15

Similarly, Jesus' question, "But whom say ye that I am?" is equally a question gauging whether His disciples believed John, Moses and the prophets.

Did Jesus' disciples understand the testimony of the prophets?

Hear Simon Peter's answer:

16. And Simon Peter answered and said, Thou art the Christ, the Son of the living God. 17. And Jesus answered and said unto him, Blessed art thou, Simon Barjona: for flesh and blood hath not revealed it unto thee, but my Father which is in heaven. 18. And I say also unto thee, That thou art Peter, and upon this rock I will build my church; and the gates of hell shall not prevail against it.
Matthew 16:16-18

Peter's answer was "Thou art the Christ, the Son of the living God."

Jesus' "flesh and blood hath not revealed it unto thee" means that Peter had not responded like the people who had rumoured that Jesus was either John the Baptist, Elias, Jeremias, or one of the prophets.

So how had Peter come about this revelation? We see its origin in Andrew's words:

41. He first findeth his own brother Simon, and saith unto him, We have found the Messias, which is, being interpreted, the Christ.
John 1:41

It was Andrew who had informed Peter about John's message concerning Jesus.

What had John the Baptist taught Andrew?

36. And looking upon Jesus as he walked, he saith, Behold the Lamb of God!
John 1:36

So, when Andrew told Peter "we have found the Messias," he was conveying John's "behold the Lamb of God!". Peter therefore had also heard John preach that Jesus was the Lamb of God.

Philip had told these same facts to Nathanael as, "we have found him, of whom Moses in the law, and the prophets, did write, Jesus of Nazareth, the son of Joseph".

So, John had preached from the writings of Moses in the law and the prophets, which is what Andrew would have used to inform Peter about what John had said of Jesus.

Peter had seen who Jesus was from the writings of Moses in the law, and the writings of the prophets.

> *17. And Jesus answered and said unto him, Blessed art thou, Simon Barjona: for flesh and blood hath not revealed it unto thee, but my Father which is in heaven.*
> *Matthew 16:17*

What did Jesus mean by "my Father which is in heaven"?

"My Father which is in heaven" would be the Father, who by His spirit, had inspired Moses in the law and the prophets to write down their prophecies concerning Jesus as the Lamb of God. It was via John's teaching of the writings of Moses and the prophets that Peter had come in contact with the truth of who Jesus was. Thus, this "Father in heaven" is a figurative acknowledgment that Peter had bypassed the rumors of the people by speaking in the light of John's testimony.

By affirming Peter's mighty confession "thou art the Christ, the Son of the living God," the Lord Jesus validated the testimony of John, Moses and the prophets as Father-given revelation. Peter had not arrived at this understanding by listening to the senses.

The gates of hell shall not prevail

The expression "the gates of hell" is a Semitic figure of speech for the realm of death. The Semitic people believed that when a person died, he or she was ushered into the world of death. On entering, the gates were shut so that the dead could not get back to the world of life. Thus, "the gates of hell" referred to the permanence of death. The only way to get out of death would be by resurrection.

The gate refers to the power or authority of death.

The phrase "prevail against" Matthew 16:18 is a Greek word meaning "to be superior in strength", "to overcome or to be strong to another's detriment".

When Jesus said, "I will build my church; and the gates of hell shall not prevail against it", He meant that the power of death would not prevail, prevent, be superior to, or hinder Jesus coming out of the realm of death by His resurrection. This meant that the "My church" Jesus built was His resurrection from the dead.

The church is proof that the power or authority of death is destroyed in the resurrection of Jesus.

In 1 Corinthians 15:56, Paul shows that this "power of death" is also known as the sting of death, which is sin. Regarding the power of death, the writer of Hebrews also says:

14. Forasmuch then as the children are partakers of flesh and blood, he also himself likewise took part of the same; that through death he might destroy him that had the power of death, that is, the devil;
15. And deliver them who through fear of death were all their lifetime subject to bondage.
Hebrews 2:14-15

The adversary, the devil had the power of death. "He also himself likewise took part of the same" refers to the fact that God was found as a man in His incarnation.

The phrase "he might destroy" in Hebrews 2:14 is translated from a Greek word also meaning "to render idle", "to unemploy", and "to deprive of force". The writer of Hebrews wants us to know that in His sacrifice, Jesus has destroyed him that "had the power of death." Since, this "power of death" is sin, the power of death, which is the gates of hell, had no mastery over the sacrifice of Christ. In building His church, Jesus' would deal with the sin issue.

Here's what John said regarding hell and death:

18. I am he that liveth, and was dead; and, behold, I am alive for evermore, Amen; and have the keys of hell and of death.
Revelation 1:18

In His death, Jesus entered the realm of the dead. However, His expression, "I am he that liveth and was dead" means that He that died is no longer dead but now alive. This is the resurrection. By His resurrection, Jesus has taken the keys of hell and of death.

Therefore, the expressions "keys of hell and of death", "the power of death" and "the gates of hell" are one and the same. Jesus overcame or disarmed that power by His resurrection. This means that Jesus had the resurrection in view when He taught "the gates of hell shall not prevail against it."

What will the gates of hell not prevail against?

The gates of hell shall not prevail against "I will build My church."

Therefore, the resurrection is how Jesus built His church!

Not possible that He should be held of death

24. Whom God hath raised up, having loosed the pains of death: because it was not possible that he should be holden of it. 25. For David speaketh concerning him, I foresaw the Lord always before my face, for he is on my right hand, that I should not be moved: 26. Therefore did my heart rejoice, and my tongue was glad; moreover also my flesh shall rest in hope: 27. Because thou wilt not leave my soul in hell, neither wilt thou suffer thine Holy One to see corruption. 28. Thou hast made known to me the ways of life; thou shalt make me full of joy with thy countenance. 29. Men and brethren, let me freely speak unto you of the patriarch David, that he is both dead and buried, and his sepulchre is with us unto this day. 30. Therefore being a prophet, and knowing that God had sworn with an oath to him, that of the fruit of his loins, according to the flesh, he would raise up Christ to sit on his throne; 31. He seeing this before spake of the resurrection of Christ, that his soul was not left in hell, neither his flesh did see corruption. 32. This Jesus hath God raised up, whereof we all are witnesses.
Acts 2:24-32

Peter explains that God had promised David that Jesus would not be kept in the dominion of death. Observe how God had loosed the pains of death in that He raised Jesus from the dead. God personally prevailed against the gates of hell. This is God's glory alone in that He is responsible for the resurrection of Jesus.

I will build My church

> *18. And I say also unto thee, That thou art Peter, and upon this rock I will build my church; and the gates of hell shall not prevail against it.*
> *Matthew 16:18*

The expression "I will build" in "I will build my church" is one word in Greek. It means "to lay a foundation", "to establish", "to erect a building" or "to build a house".

Thus, Jesus is doing a work which death will not be superior. In other words, Jesus' work would be His superiority over the power of death.

This means that when Jesus speaks of "My church" He is prophesying of His resurrection.

His resurrection is "My church." It is His work. His signature. His distinguishing act, which is unstoppable by the gates of hell.

His resurrection is His work of erecting His building.

What did Jesus build in His resurrection?

> *22. But ye are come unto mount Sion, and unto the city of the living God, the heavenly Jerusalem, and to an innumerable company of angels, 23. To the general assembly and church of the firstborn, which are written in heaven, and to God the Judge of all, and to the spirits of just men made perfect,*
> *Hebrews 12:22-23*

Take note of that expression, "the church of the firstborn".

18. And he is the head of the body, the church: who is the beginning, the firstborn from the dead; that in all things he might have the preeminence.
Colossians 1:18

Jesus is the firstborn from the dead. Jesus as firstborn from the dead is the same One over whom the power of death was destroyed. Jesus the firstborn is Jesus the resurrected One. His being Firstborn is in His resurrection.

It is also in His resurrection as the firstborn that He is referred to as "the head of the body, the church." The body is how Paul refers to the chief result of Christ's resurrection.

Jesus, the head, produced the body in the resurrection. This body is not His skin. Paul identifies the church as the body Jesus produced in the resurrection.

The resurrection of Jesus is the building of His body.

This body is the church. This is the work that He built.

The church is His body in the resurrection. The body is the completeness that Jesus accomplished in His resurrection. He built what He had said He would build by rising from the dead. The resurrection of Jesus is so total and complete that it cannot be added to or improved.

First, we gave Jesus our human body, when He became a man. Afterwards, men put Him to death in the body that men gave Him.
In the grand finale, His resurrection is His work, by which He gives us His body, which we become a part of once we believe the gospel.

Jesus is risen. He has built His church, which is His body. We have believed and received the gift of His body.

In His building, over which the gates of hell could not prevail, He built a body. Since, one that builds or produces a body is the head or source of the body, then Jesus is the head of the body.

The writer of Hebrews says that the one that believes has come unto mount Sion, which is "the general assembly and church of the first-born".

The General assembly is the church of the firstborn.

The church of the firstborn is Jesus' "My church."

The word translated "assembly" in "the general assembly and church" is from a Greek word that also means festival.

The writer of Hebrews speaks of an innumerable company of angels, which the writer later refers to as "the spirits of just men made perfect." Thus, this "general assembly" is a company of men rejoicing in celebration or festivity. The resurrection of Jesus is presented as a festival. This celebration is the resurrection.

The writer of Hebrews further explains that believers in the gospel come together in the resurrection of Jesus. It is not another resurrection but the same preached in Christ. As believers, we are introduced into this body and receive His resurrection, which is His body, as our identity.

Furthermore:

12. Saying, I will declare thy name unto my brethren, in the midst of the church will I sing praise unto thee.
Hebrews 2:12

The writer of Hebrews is teaching from Psalm 22:22.

The church is Jesus' body the fulness of Him in the resurrection. "In the midst of the church" is not talking about our church meetings but "My church" that Jesus built in His resurrection.

To "declare thy name unto my brethren" is to preach or announce Jesus's work or His accomplishment. In His accomplishment, over which the gates of hell could not prevail, He produced a body. The one that produces a body is the head or source of the body. Thus, Jesus is the head of the body. Jesus is the head of that body (His work in resurrection). This resurrection, which He had called "My church" is then declared or preached to us, and we are His brethren in that resurrection.

When we believe the truth of His resurrection ("My church"), nothing in death or hell can stop us being assembled in that one body.

11. For both he that sanctifieth and they who are sanctified are all of one: for which cause he is not ashamed to call them brethren,
Hebrews 2:11

His resurrection is His sanctification, which was preached unto us. We believed it, and we received His resurrection as our sanctification in His. His resurrection is how He served us.

13. And again, I will put my trust in him. And again, Behold I and the children which God hath given me.
Hebrews 2:13

The writer of Hebrews is teaching from Isaiah 8:18, a passage that gives us a glimpse of Jesus' thoughts in redemption.

"Behold I and the children which God hath given me" is the fulfilment of Isaiah's "I and the children which God hath given me we are for signs and wonders."

The "wonders" is what Jesus had explained as "I will build My church."

The wonder is Christ building His body in His resurrection. "I and the children that the Lord has given me" means that there are brethren that assemble in the resurrection of Jesus.

He shared in our body so that He could do His work of rising from the dead. That sharing was a sign of His resurrection, in which He gives us His body to share in.

18. And I say also unto thee, That thou art Peter, and upon this rock I will build my church; and the gates of hell shall not prevail against it.
Matthew 16:18

This building is Christ's work done in His resurrection.

4. There is one body, and one Spirit, even as ye are called in one hope of your calling;
Ephesians 4:4

The one body and one Spirit are not two different ideas. The expression is better rendered "one body, by which I refer to one Spirit". In simpler terms, the one body is the one spirit, which is the one calling.

There is one body, which is the one spirit. This is the call.

Paul's point is that the one body is His gift to us because, in the gospel, we are called into that body. What He gave is the body of Christ!

The body of Christ is that building which Jesus had said that He would build. It is Jesus' house; which Jesus has built as the fulness of His resurrection.

"My church", which is His resurrection refers to His spirit, which is the one spirit that makes up His people.

John records another instance where Jesus had taught about His work:

I will raise it up

19. Jesus answered and said unto them, Destroy this temple, and in three days I will raise it up.
John 2:19

What is this temple that Jesus promised to raise up in three days?

John clarifies:

21. But he spake of the temple of his body. 22. When therefore he was risen from the dead, his disciples remembered that he had said this unto them; and they believed the scripture, and the word which Jesus had said.
John 2:21-22

"His disciples remembered" refers to the understanding that the disciples had after Jesus explained it following His resurrection. It was in Jesus' explanation that the disciples understood that He spoke of the temple of His body.

So, "I raise" in "in three days I raise it up" refers to His work in the resurrection. It means that by His resurrection the Lord Jesus will produce His body.

The Head and His body the church

20. Which he wrought in Christ, when he raised him from the dead, and set him at his own right hand in the heavenly places, 21. Far above all principality, and power, and might, and dominion, and every name that is named, not only in this world, but also in that which is to come: 22. And hath put all things under his feet, and gave him to be the head over all things to the church,23. Which is his body, the fulness of him that filleth all in all.
Ephesians 1:22-23

In this portion of scripture Paul teaches about the resurrection power which God used to raise Christ from the dead. In that resurrection, Jesus is the head of the church. The body of Christ is seen in His resurrection. Whatever happened to Christ happened to the body of Christ. The church is from the resurrection. It is His body.

The expression "gave Him" in "gave him to be the head over all things to the church" describes Jesus's resurrection, for His resurrection is God's gift.

Where do we see what God has given?

We see what God has given in His body the church. So the church is Christ expressed amongst men on the earth.

Paul explains that the church is "His body, the fulness of Him". The word translated fulness is from a Greek word that refers to "the complete thing". His fulness is everything about Him. His body as the fulness of Him means that His resurrection is the measure of all that He did and apart from which He did nothing. That resurrection completes us in Him.

10. He that descended is the same also that ascended up far above all heavens, that he might fill all things.)
Ephesians 4:10

Jesus fills all things in His resurrection.

"The body of Christ" is His fulness that nothing can make any fuller, for it is the mighty work of His resurrection.

30. He serves and satisfies us as members of his body
Ephesians 5:30 (TPT)

Our membership of His body is not biological but spiritual. That membership speaks of our union with Him. We are joined to Him in one spirit. Therefore, His body, which Paul refers to as His flesh, and His bones all refer to our joining with Him in the spirit.

5. So we, being many, are one body in Christ, and every one members one of another.
Romans 12:5

Thus, Christ only built one body, and every saint is in that one body in Christ. There are no two bodies because there are no duplicate resurrections. Jesus' one work is His one body formed in His resurrection. The one body in Christ is our joining with Him. We are one body in Christ. Whoever is not of this one body is not in the work of Christ and is therefore not saved.

He obligated Himself

18. And I say also unto thee, That thou art Peter, and upon this rock I will build my church; and the gates of hell shall not prevail against it.
Matthew 16:18

When Jesus said, "I will build my church," He was affirming the correctness of the teaching to which Peter had been exposed to. It was based on Peter's "Thou art the Christ, the Son of the living God," that Jesus said, "I will build my church." Jesus was using the scriptures to teach a fuller explanation of what Peter had heard John teach.

The word that has been translated "church" in "I will build my church" is the Greek ekklēsia, meaning "congregation." As used in the scriptures, ekklēsia refers to any assembly of people for any reason. In its wider usage in scriptures, the reason for the gathering is not necessarily religious.

For instance, Luke explains an uproar against Paul's ministry in Asia:

32. Some therefore cried one thing, and some another: for the assembly was confused; and the more part knew not wherefore they were come together.
Acts 19:32

Here, the word "assembly" is the same word that is usually translated as "church" – ekklēsia. In this passage, the assembly (church) refers to the coming together of a mob in which some "cried one thing, and some another." So, it refers to a crowd who could not agree on why they were gathered!

Another example as Stephen preached,

38. This is he, that was in the church in the wilderness with the angel which spake to him in the mount Sina, and with our fathers: who received the lively oracles to give unto us:
Acts 7:38

In this passage, "church" referred to the Jews and the mixed multitude who had been led out of Egypt by Moses (see Exodus 12:37-38, Numbers 11:4). This mixed multitude was made up of non-Jews.

Thus, in the scriptures, the terms "assembly", "church", and other renditions of ekklēsia do not have a fixed meaning. Most importantly, we see that the term "church" is not only used for Christians. We let the setting determine its meaning.

Notwithstanding the variety in the use of the word ekklēsia in the bible, in the Matthew 16 passage, Jesus has a specific meaning in mind, for He speaks of "My church." By saying "my church" He wants His hearers to know that subject is very personal to Him.

Jesus would be teaching His disciples from the Law of Moses and the prophets. His teaching is "I will build." He does not say, "I continue to build." This means that once He builds, it is done and remains done and would not be visited again.

"I will build" means that He will personally bring it to pass. It is not something that He will delegate to another. This is a promise. It is a prophecy of what Jesus would do in the resurrection. This is what He will be identified as – the builder or the head of His church.

The Head has produced the body

23. For the husband is the head of the wife, even as Christ is the head of the church: and he is the saviour of the body.
Ephesians 5:23

Paul is explaining the same Christ that John had taught Andrew and Andrew had told Peter (see John 1:41). This is the same Christ that Philip had told Nathanael "We have found him, of whom Moses in the law, and the prophets, did write" (see John 1:45)

Thus, it is from the writings of Moses in the law, and the writings of the prophets that Paul understood that as Saviour of the body, Christ is the head of the church.

The Greek word translated "and" between "the head of the church" and "the Saviour of the body" is kai, which can join two distinct ideas or use one idea to further explain another idea. In this case, "the Saviour of the body" is the explanation of "the head of the church." Christ as the head of the church and Christ as the Saviour of the body is one and the same. The teaching that Christ is the head of the church means that the church came from Him.

Christ the Head has produced the body that He promised to raise up. The gift of Christ is Christ Himself in whose resurrection we have ours.

Christ the head and His body are one. It is the work Christ did in the resurrection. The term "body of Christ" is union with Christ. The salvation Christ has supplied means that His resurrection is equally true of all that believe in Him.

18. And he is the head of the body, the church: who is the beginning, the firstborn from the dead; that in all things he might have the preeminence.
Colossians 1:18

Head and body are repeatedly used referring to Christ and the church, in the context of the resurrection. In this usage, head means source. The point is that the body came from the head. The singular resurrection of the head produced the body. His body is His work as the head. It is not Christ as one thing and His body as another. He is not a monster. Rather, we are His assembly who are joined to Him. Therefore, Christ and His body are one and the same (see 1 Corinthians 6:17).

In observing Christ, we observe who He has made us in Him. As the head, Christ the son produced His body as sons. As a servant, He produced His body as servants.

Christ said He would build His church; by His resurrection, He has done exactly that.

The Universal Church

What is the call?

9. God is faithful, by whom ye were called unto the fellowship of his Son Jesus Christ our Lord.
1 Corinthians 1:9

The Greek word that has been translated fellowship means supply. God supplied His Son as the resurrected One. In His resurrection, He (the Son) built His church.

The call is into the fellowship of His Son, with the Son giving Himself to us as the gift of resurrection. Thus, this call is in the resurrection of Jesus.

26. For ye see your calling, brethren, how that not many wise men after the flesh, not many mighty, not many noble, are called:
1 Corinthians 1: 26

In the previous verses, Paul had been discussing the preaching of Christ as the power of God to save. "Your calling" refers to the preaching of Christ as the One that God has raised from the dead. Therefore, it is salvation that is referred to as calling. The called are those who have believed the preaching of Christ as the One that God has raised from the dead:

29. For whom he did foreknow, he also did predestinate to be conformed to the image of his Son, that he might be the firstborn among many brethren. 30. Moreover whom he did predestinate, them he also called: and whom he called, them he also justified: and whom he justified, them he also glorified.
Romans 8:29-30

So, God has called us by His grace to be conformed to the image of his Son, who is the firstborn among many brethren. This is the call through the gospel preached unto men.

Again, we see that God's provision of salvation is His call.

15. But when it pleased God, who separated me from my mother's womb, and called me by his grace,
Galatians 1:15

Paul affirmed that God called him by His grace. This is the gospel call.

The call of His grace is the call of salvation, the Gospel call.

What is the call out of?

9. But ye are a chosen generation, a royal priesthood, an holy nation, a peculiar people; that ye should shew forth the praises of him who hath called you out of darkness into his marvellous light:
1 Peter 2:9

It is a call out of the darkness.

8. For ye were sometimes darkness, but now are ye light in the Lord: walk as children of light:
Ephesians 5:8

The world is darkness (see also 2 Corinthians 6:14)

6. For God, who commanded the light to shine out of darkness, hath shined in our hearts, to give the light of the knowledge of the glory of God in the face of Jesus Christ.
2 Corinthians 4:6

"God, who commanded the light to shine out of darkness" is how Paul explains Moses' gospel in Genesis 1. In this explanation, we see that this darkness into which the light of the gospel shines is in the hearts of men.

14. Be ye not unequally yoked together with unbelievers: for what fellowship hath righteousness with unrighteousness? and what communion hath light with darkness?
2 Corinthians 6:14

Those who have not accepted that resurrection are called darkness for they have not accepted Christ's work.

What is the call into?

9. But ye are a chosen generation, a royal priesthood, an holy nation, a peculiar people; that ye should shew forth the praises of him who hath called you out of darkness into his marvellous light:
1 Peter 2:9

We have been called into His marvellous light. In this marvellous light, we are made a royal priesthood and a holy nation.

Thus, by believing the gospel call, you received God's holiness as a holy nation. "Nation" means everyone that has believed is holy. It is a characteristic of those who have received the call.

In the scriptures, holy vessels are made by men but dedicated for God's use. Scriptural holiness has nothing to do with some special characteristic of the vessel. It is God that has determined that the vessel is special. What God says is special is really special.

Even the holy of holies was not made in some mysterious dimension or some other planet but on earth and anyone could go there. But once completed, when men recognised it as holy, not everyone could go there. At that point, it became inaccessible.

The company of saints as "holy nation" is set by God as belonging to God. We are holy because He set us apart or sanctified us by His spirit (see 1 Corinthians 6:11).

Since by giving us His spirit, God had made us holy, then it is God that sets us as holy. We are holy unto Him. This holiness is what He has done to us in setting us apart as special to Himself as those that received the resurrection of Jesus because we have believed the gospel. We have received the call into His marvellous light.

What is this marvellous light?

9. But you are a chosen people, a royal priesthood, a holy nation, God's special possession, that you may declare the praises of him who called you out of darkness into his wonderful light:
1 Peter 2:9 (NIV)

23. That Christ should suffer, and that he should be the first that should rise from the dead, and should shew light unto the people, and to the Gentiles.
Acts 26:23

Observe that it is in His resurrection that Christ gave "light unto the people, and to the Gentiles". This light is Christ's gift of Himself in the resurrection, supplying membership in His building, His church.

Those who receive that resurrection are referred to as light (see 2 Corinthians 6:16). Those who have not accepted Christ's resurrection are without His light and are therefore called darkness.

24. Who now rejoice in my sufferings for you, and fill up that which is behind of the afflictions of Christ in my flesh for his body's sake, which is the church:
Colossians 1:24

His body is the same as the Church, and both are used interchange-ably:

> *27. Now ye are the body of Christ, and members in particular.*
> *1 Corinthians 12:27*

Instead of "Now ye are the body of Christ" we can say "now ye are the church." All that have received God's gift of salvation belong in the body of Christ.

In the King James, Ye is not singular. It is a plural word in old English. It refers to a collective. When we believed the gospel, we received our membership in the work Christ had done. He assembled us in Him. We are therefore the body of Christ.

> *12. For as the body is one, and hath many members, and all the members of*
> *that one body, being many, are one body: so also is Christ.*
> *1 Corinthians 12:12*

Paul's expressions "as the body is one" and "so also is Christ" shows that he is comparing two bodies. He uses the natural human body (the body is one) to explain Christ's body. According to Paul's analogy, just as the natural human body has many members, the same is true of Christ.

In Paul's teaching about the saint being the body of Christ, he does not proceed to further divide the body by its parts and then refer to saints as a specific part of the body. We are not following the teaching of Paul if we then say that some saints are the mouth, others the eye, and others some other part of the body.

The body of Christ is a coming together in Christ, with others who, by hearing and believing the gospel have been called out of darkness into the marvellous light.

The church is a holy nation

9. But you are a chosen race, a royal priesthood, a holy nation, a people of his
own, so that you may proclaim the virtues of the one who called you out of
darkness into his marvelous light
1 Peter 2:9 (NET)

The Church is another nation other than the various people grouping that we came from (the nations). Rather, since the church is holy by God's choice, then we the Church are not the nations (heathen), who have not believed the gospel.

The believer is made of that holy nation on account of believing the gospel. The heathen has not received the gospel. The heathen is not of that holy nation. Therefore, the bible term nation refers to the unity of men in responding alike to the gospel by believing its message.

The Church is a distinct culture governed by the resurrection of Christ. It is the culture of God's love seen in the sacrifice of Christ. It is the one nation that God is associated with on the earth, His holy nation.

The fact of the church as a distinct nation is seen elsewhere in Paul's writings:

32. Give none offence, neither to the Jews, nor to the Gentiles, nor to the church
of God:
1 Corinthians 10:32

In His resurrection, Christ built His church, and in the light of that resurrection, we do not only speak of Jews and Gentiles. We recognize a distinction called the church of God.

Those that accept the gospel are in the church. To the Jew, these people that believe the gospel are still Jews. To the Gentiles, they are still Gentiles. However, in the eyes of God, they are the church that God has built in the resurrection of Christ.

So the distinction that God created between men is in relation to the gospel. There are two types of men – those that believe the gospel and those that do not. All those that believe the gospel are the holy nation.

God's answer is to showcase the church as His tribe.

Why the Jew?

4. Who are Israelites; to whom pertaineth the adoption, and the glory, and the covenants, and the giving of the law, and the service of God, and the promises; 5. Whose are the fathers, and of whom as concerning the flesh Christ came, who is over all, God blessed for ever. Amen. 6. Not as though the word of God hath taken none effect. For they are not all Israel, which are of Israel:
Romans 9:4-6

In other words, Christ is God's intention. He is the target that God had always had in mind, the special product that came out of Israel and the reason for and fulfilment of Israel.

The purpose of the Jews was that they were custodians of the truth of God and through them, after the flesh, the Saviour would be born. The promise of God would not be fulfilled by the Jew but by that holy One.

15. Having abolished in his flesh the enmity, even the law of commandments contained in ordinances; for to make in himself of twain one new man, so making peace;
Ephesians 2:15

The enmity is the law of commandments, which is man's trust in rituals. It is the big lie that by keeping those ordinances, men added Christ to their lives as a reward for obedience.

This is man's unbelief.

The term "of twain" means of the two – a division. Man's unbelief created artificial distinctions between the Jew, who observed the rituals, and the Gentiles that did not.

In the resurrection, Christ has built one man in Christ. This is His work in redemption. This "one new man" is the measure of God's power in redemption.

16. And that he might reconcile both unto God in one body by the cross, having slain the enmity thereby: 17. And came and preached peace to you which were afar off, and to them that were nigh. 18. For through him we both have access by one Spirit unto the Father.
Ephesians 2:16-18

Rather than believe in God's promise, the Jew trusted in their performance of their rituals, referring to those who do not trust in their rituals as uncircumcised. These are the Gentiles. They created an artificial division between men.

Jesus has broken down that distinction called "Jews and Gentiles." He has abolished the middle wall of partition. Jesus' work that had been called one new man in verse 15 of Ephesians 2, is now described as "one body" in verse 16 and "one Spirit" in verse 18. This is the tribe of believers assembled by God in the holy nation.

The term "we both" refers to the Jew and Gentile. The man that believes is called out of "Jew and Gentile" into the holy nation.

Our access to God is not via our tribes as Jews or Gentiles but via the God-created tribe, which Paul calls "one spirit" or "one body," which is the church.

32. Give none offence, neither to the Jews, nor to the Gentiles, nor to the church of God:
1 Corinthians 10:32

In his revelation, Paul distinguishes between Jew, Gentile, and Church of God. The church is the assembly in the resurrection of Jesus. As used here, the Jew and Gentile have their own culture and they are united in that they are not believers in Christ's resurrection. The man that believes the gospel is called out of the nation of "Jews and Gentiles" into the assembly in the church of God. So the church of God is in the midst of Jews and Gentiles" but is distinct from them by the resurrection of Jesus.

Alive forever more

> *18. And I say also unto thee, That thou art Peter, and upon this rock I will build my church; and the gates of hell shall not prevail against it.*
> *Matthew 16:18*

The Church did not exist until Jesus built it, not before Christ's sacrifice and His resurrection.

The word "church" was translated from the Greek word that means "to call out."

> *18. He is the Head of his body, which is the church. And since he is the beginning and the firstborn heir in resurrection, he is the most exalted One, holding first place in everything.*
> *Colossians 1:18 (TPT)*

Christ is "the head of the body, the church." The Church refers to the entire world congregation of Christians and all those who have believed in Christ through the ages.

> *22. But ye are come unto mount Sion, and unto the city of the living God, the heavenly Jerusalem, and to an innumerable company of angels, 23. To the general assembly and church of the firstborn, which are written in heaven, and to God the Judge of all, and to the spirits of just men made perfect,*
> *Hebrews 12:22-23*

The church of the firstborn is the general assembly.

The man that believes the gospel has come to Zion, the church of the firstborn, which is the one body that all saints of all ages belong to. All those who hoped in Christ before He came as well as all who have believed the gospel of the resurrection are of this one body.

There is one body

3 Make every effort to keep the unity of the Spirit through the bond of peace.
4 There is one body and one Spirit, just as you were called to one hope when you
were called;
Ephesians 4:3-4 (NIV)

Paul told the Ephesians about the unity of the Spirit. The one spirit is the one body – the universal church.

The Lord our God shall call

38. Then Peter said unto them, Repent, and be baptized every one of you in the name of Jesus Christ for the remission of sins, and ye shall receive the gift of the Holy Ghost. 39. For the promise is unto you, and to your children, and to all that are afar off, even as many as the Lord our God shall call.
Acts 2:38-39

What was Peter doing? He was preaching to men.

What was he preaching? Peter preached the good news, which is the fact that God had raised Jesus from the dead (see Acts 2:32).

What is the promise? The promise is the gift of the Holy Ghost.

Who is the promise for? The promise is for "you, and to your children, and to all that are afar off, even as many as the Lord our God shall call".

What are the men to receive? Men are to receive this gift of the Holy Ghost.

Thus, the work of God amongst men is that through the preaching of the gospel, those that believe receive the gift of the Holy Ghost. By this, they are in the church of God.

How would we know all that believe Jesus? They would all receive the promise of the spirit from the Father.

In hearing the gospel, we receive the promise of His spirit. This Spirit is membership in God's family.

Luke described further:

> *47. praising God and having the good will of all the people. And the Lord was adding to their number every day those who were being saved.*
> *Acts 2:47 (NET)*

The Lord added to the church by the ministry of the men who preached the gospel. The men that receive the spirit are the ones that have membership in the church. Thus, His work gives us the spirit, which is membership in the body of Christ, which is the church of God.

We are one family

> *19. Now therefore ye are no more strangers and foreigners, but fellowcitizens with the saints, and of the household of God;*
> *Ephesians 2:19*

Earlier in Ephesians 2, Paul had described Jesus' work as "one new man" (verse 15), and "one body" (verse 16) and "one Spirit" (verse 18) is now referred to as the household of God.

All those who have received the gift of God's spirit by believing in the resurrection of Jesus are the holy nation, which is the household of God. As God's household, we are one tribe. We are the same household. We are the Father's family. Although, from the natural standpoint, we are from different tribes, in Christ we are one family in His resurrection.

> *10. So then, whenever we have an opportunity, let us do good to all people, and especially to those who belong to the family of faith.*
> *Galatians 6:10 (NET)*

The KJV's "household of faith" is the house or family built in the faithfulness of God, who raised Christ from the dead. It describes all the men and women who have received God's faithfulness in the resurrection of Jesus.

Paul taught the truth of "the household of God" to the Galatians as "the household of faith". The terms, Church, household of God, and household of faith are not three different families but one. Therefore, whether in Galatia, Ephesus, Colosse, Corinth, Rome, Antioch, or Thessalonica, all the saints, irrespective of their location, belong to the same spiritual household, which is the church, the body of Christ.

The only organization in the universal church is that the Lord Jesus is the head and that all in that body believe in the resurrection. It is one entity of which Christ is the head.

No one can physically identify the universal church. The universal church does not pray, study the Word, preach, or measure its progress in reaching the world with the gospel.

What is the local assembly?

13. For by one Spirit are we all baptized into one body, whether we be Jews or Gentiles, whether we be bond or free; and have been all made to drink into one Spirit.
1 Corinthians 12:13

The expression "have been all made to drink into one Spirit" means that all the saints have the spirit in common.

All who believe the gospel are identified with Jesus and they exist in the work of Christ. They are united with Him in that they are quickened together, raised together, seated together because He indwells each by His indwelling spirit.

The church is the body of Christ. The church came into being by Jesus' act of resurrection from the dead. All those that believe the gospel gather in Him as Saviour. This is one body. He is the Saviour of the body. This is in the spirit.

The thing to note is that the church as the body of Christ is universal, spiritual, and invisible.

However, there is another expression in the bible. The church at a place.

Another use of Ekklēsia

Observe the following texts:

I will build my church (See Matthew 16:18).

Christ is the head of the church: (See Ephesians 5:23).

The church is subject unto Christ (See Ephesians 5:24).

I speak concerning Christ and the church (See Ephesians 5:32).

He is the head of the body, the church (See Colossians 1:18).

The head over all things to the church (See Ephesians 1:22).

And now observe this:

2. To the church of God in Corinth, to those sanctified in Christ Jesus and called to be his holy people, together with all those everywhere who call on the name of our Lord Jesus Christ—their Lord and ours:
1 Corinthians 1:2 (NIV)

Jesus sanctified us in His resurrection, by which He gave the gift of His spirit. We are holy because He set us apart or sanctified us by His spirit

When a man hears the gospel, he receives this spirit as sanctification in Christ Jesus. The sanctified in Christ are "all those everywhere who call on the name of our Lord Jesus Christ." All believers received His resurrection as our sanctification in His.

It is the same Greek word Ekklēsia that has been translated "church" in Matthew 16:18, Ephesians 5:23,24,32;1:22, and Colossians 1:18 that has been translated "church" in "the church of God which is at Corinth."

Who is Paul addressing in this Epistle?

He says it is "the church of God in Corinth." That phrase "in Corinth" is noteworthy. The church which by definition is universal, spiritual, and invisible is now identified with a specific place.

That place is Corinth. Corinth is not universal, spiritual, or invisible.

1. Paul, an apostle of Jesus Christ by the will of God, and Timothy our brother, unto the church of God which is at Corinth, with all the saints which are in all Achaia:
2 Corinthians 1:1

Here Paul repeats his expression "the church of God which is at Corinth." This time he includes "the saints which are in all Achaia."

Both Achaia and Corinth are physical locations. The church of God, which is in the resurrection of Christ is now said to be in a physical place.

2. And all the brethren which are with me, unto the churches of Galatia:
Galatians 1:2

In this passage, Paul does not repeat his expression "the church of God which is at Corinth." Instead, he says, "the churches of Galatia". Had he stuck with "the church of God which is at Corinth," we might have considered it as a figure of speech. However, Paul does not use the singular "church of Galatia"; rather, He speaks of a plurality of churches!

The church over which Christ is head is singular and spiritual. Now Paul speaks of the churches. Does he mean there are many resurrections or that Christ died and rose again multiple times in order to produce many churches? No, there is only one resurrection and only one body of Christ.

Galatia is a physical region. The expression "the churches of Galatia" shows that there were many churches in Galatia.

22. And was unknown by face unto the churches of Judaea which were in
Christ:
Galatians 1:22

Paul here speaks of the "the churches of Judaea", which are different and separate from the "churches of Galatia" that he had mentioned earlier. The term "churches of Judaea" refers to all the pockets of churches throughout Judea. He is clearly describing something different from the singular, universal, spiritual, and invisible Church, which Christ built in His resurrection.

3. Greet Priscilla and Aquila my helpers in Christ Jesus: 4. Who have for my
life laid down their own necks: unto whom not only I give thanks, but also all
the churches of the Gentiles. 5. Likewise greet the church that is in their house.
Salute my wellbeloved Epaenetus, who is the firstfruits of Achaia unto Christ.
Romans 16:3-5

Paul speaks of "all the churches of the Gentiles." Although it is the same Greek word that has been used to describe the singular, universal, spiritual, and invisible church, Paul's use of "churches" lets us know that he is most definitely referring to something asides the universal church. There is no way the universal church can fit into the house of Priscilla and Aquila.

Then speaking of Priscilla and Aquila, he speaks of another "church that is in their house." The term "church that is in their house" means that the house of Priscilla and Aquila is where you see the church that Paul speaks of.

If one were to go check the house of Priscilla and Aquila, this assembly of saints that Paul calls the church, would be seen in fellowship.

Whereas, when Paul says:

29. For no man ever yet hated his own flesh; but nourisheth and cherisheth it,
even as the Lord the church: 30. For we are members of his body, of his flesh,
and of his bones.
Ephesians 5:29-30

This church that we are members of "his body, of his flesh, and of his bones" is spiritual. Our eyes do not see this. Our eyes would have seen the church in the house of Priscilla and Aquila.

1. I commend unto you Phebe our sister, which is a servant of the church which is
at Cenchrea:
Romans 16:1

Paul speaks of Phoebe who serves in "the church which is at Cenchrea". This church at Cenchrea is distinct from the church that is in the house of Priscilla and Aquila.

23. As for Titus, he is my partner and co-worker among you; as for our brothers,
they are representatives of the churches and an honor to Christ.
2 Corinthians 8:23 (NIV)

Paul affirms that Titus and some other ministers are "the messengers of the churches"

Again, Paul's use of "churches" lets us know that he is most definitely referring to something asides the universal church, which is one. It also shows that he had many local churches in mind.

1 Paul, a prisoner of Christ Jesus, and Timothy our brother, To Philemon our
dear friend and fellow worker— 2 also to Apphia our sister and Archippus our
fellow soldier—and to the church that meets in your home:
Philemon 1:1-2 (NIV)

Paul is speaking of Philemon in this verse. When he speaks of "church in thy house", Paul means that Philemon's house is where you see the church that Paul speaks of. Paul is speaking of a specific set of people in Colosse. He does not imply that Philemon has found a way to fit the universal church into his house.

Taken together, we see from Paul's usage that the Greek word translated church, ekklēsia is used to describe the practice of saints who share in the resurrection coming together in a place to express that invisible assembly in the resurrection of Christ. These are a specific local assembly of believers. It is this gathering in one place that we refer to as the local body, the local assembly, or the local church.

On account of this unseen, invisible but rich body, this visible gathering of men is the consequence of the gathering that happened in the resurrection of Jesus.

Here's what John said in his Epistle:

> *10. Wherefore, if I come, I will remember his deeds which he doeth, prating against us with malicious words: and not content therewith, neither doth he himself receive the brethren, and forbiddeth them that would, and casteth them out of the church.*
> *3 John 1:10*

John warns about Diotrephes, who does not receive the brethren, hinders those who want to receive those he has refused to receive and "casteth them out of the church."

Does the expression, "casteth them out of the church" mean that Diotrephes could overpower Jesus by throwing men out of the body of Christ, which Jesus had built in His resurrection? Certainly not! This is not a reference to the holy nation in Christ, our universal brotherhood.

To cast or throw "them out of the church" speaks of a particular local assembly of believers where the saints are gathered and where men like Diotrephes wield enough influence to throw other saints out. This church of which John speaks is not the universal church.

Unfortunately, there are more people who readily admit the truth of the one body than there are those who recognize the equally important truth of the local assembly.

The seven churches of Revelation

Here's further insight from John in Revelation:

4. John to the seven churches which are in Asia: Grace be unto you, and peace,
from him which is, and which was, and which is to come; and from the seven
Spirits which are before his throne;
Revelation 1:4

The expression "Grace be unto you, and peace, from him" was cus-
tomary of the apostolic greeting to the churches. By the inspiration of
God, John wrote to the 7 churches. These 7 churches which were all
in Asia, are not the one church that Christ built, against which He had
said the gates of hell cannot prevail.

Unto the angel of the church of Ephesus write; These things saith he
that holdeth the seven stars in his right hand, who walketh in the midst
of the seven golden candlesticks;
Revelation 2:1

The church of Ephesus is not that one body, that Christ built, against
which He had said the gates of hell cannot prevail. This church that
John addresses is in the city of Ephesus.

8. And unto the angel of the church in Smyrna write; These things saith the first
and the last, which was dead, and is alive;
Revelation 2:8

The church in Smyrna was not that one body, that Christ had built,
once and for all, in His resurrection. This church that John had written
to was in the city of Smyrna.

12. And to the angel of the church in Pergamos write; These things saith he
which hath the sharp sword with two edges;
Revelation 2:12

The church in Pergamos was not the church in Smyrna. It was not that
one body, that Christ built, once and for all in His resurrection. This

church that John addresses was in the city of Pergamos.

18. And unto the angel of the church in Thyatira write; These things saith the Son of God, who hath his eyes like unto a flame of fire, and his feet are like fine brass;
Revelation 2:18

This church in the city of Thyatira is not the church in any of the other six cities that John had written to, it is not universal but particular to Thyatira.

1. And unto the angel of the church in Sardis write; These things saith he that hath the seven Spirits of God, and the seven stars; I know thy works, that thou hast a name that thou livest, and art dead.
Revelation 3:1

This church in the city of Sardis is not the universal church. It is not the church in any of the other six cities. It is particular to Sardis.

7. And to the angel of the church in Philadelphia write; These things saith he that is holy, he that is true, he that hath the key of David, he that openeth, and no man shutteth; and shutteth, and no man openeth; Revelation 3:7

This church in the city of Philadelphia is not the church in any of the other six cities that John had written to, it is not universal but particular to Philadelphia.

14. And unto the angel of the church of the Laodiceans write; These things saith the Amen, the faithful and true witness, the beginning of the creation of God;
Revelation 3:14

John wrote to the same church of the Laodiceans that Paul had earlier written to.

16. And when this epistle is read among you, cause that it be read also in the
church of the Laodiceans; and that ye likewise read the epistle from Laodicea.
Colossians 4:16

Paul acknowledges that there was the church of the Laodiceans where
his epistle was to be read to the assembly. He also distinguished between "among you" and "in the church of the Laodiceans". The
church at Colosse was not the church of the Laodiceans.

Now we know that one of the scriptural reasons for the church in a
particular place was for it to serve as the place where the teachings of
the apostles are read together by the group of saints.

22. Then tidings of these things came unto the ears of the church which was in
Jerusalem: and they sent forth Barnabas, that he should go as far as Antioch.
Acts 11:22

Luke speaks of the church which was in Jerusalem, the same that sent
Barnabas to go start another church in the city of Antioch. Therefore,
the church at Jerusalem is not the church at Antioch.

1. Now there were in the church that was at Antioch certain prophets and
teachers; as Barnabas, and Simeon that was called Niger, and Lucius of
Cyrene, and Manaen, which had been brought up with Herod the tetrarch, and
Saul.
Acts 13:1

Again, Luke confirms that Barnabas started a separate church at Antioch. We also observe that the saints and leaders who were at the
church that was at Antioch were distinct from the leaders of the
church which was in Jerusalem.

What do we observe about these churches?

18. For first of all, when ye come together in the church, I hear that there be
divisions among you; and I partly believe it.
1 Corinthians 11:18

Paul affirms "when ye come together in the church." the local assembly is our coming together as saints. He did not say "if you come together". He said "when ye come together." Thus, coming together is characteristic of the local assembly.

> *17. Now in this that I declare unto you I praise you not, that ye come together*
> *not for the better, but for the worse.*
> *1 Corinthians 11:17*

We see again that the church is where "Ye come together."

> *20. When ye come together therefore into one place, this is not to eat the Lord's*
> *supper.*
> *1 Corinthians 11:20*

Paul shows that this coming together is in one place.

> *23. If therefore the whole church be come together into one place, and all speak*
> *with tongues, and there come in those that are unlearned, or unbelievers, will they*
> *not say that ye are mad?*
> *1 Corinthians 14:23*

We observe again that the whole church functions by coming together into one place. When this church gathers, unbelievers could come into the meeting place. Notice that whereas there are no unbelievers in the church that Christ built in the resurrection, unbelievers can come to this church in Corinth.

Paul's teaching is that it is the church that comes to the place. The place could very well have been a canteen prior to their coming together there. It is the thing done there that marks it out as a church.

Earlier Paul had referred to the place where they meet as the church (see 1 Corinthians 11:18). Both the people and the place can be referred to as the church.

The saints that gather in one place are the church.

Also, the church is the one place where the saints gather.

Do not forsake the assembling

24. And let us consider one another to provoke unto love and to good works: 25. Not forsaking the assembling of ourselves together, as the manner of some is; but exhorting one another: and so much the more, as ye see the day approaching.
Hebrews 10:24

All saints are members of the one body of Christ. The writer of Hebrews shows two distinct conducts seen in the saints. He says of one group that they have a manner or pattern of "forsaking the assembling of ourselves together". He then instructs the saints not to emulate that poor conduct, which forsakes the assembling of ourselves together. So the saints, who have already assembled in the resurrection of Jesus when they heard the gospel, are commanded not to forsake "the assembling of ourselves together."

Why?

It is in our practice of assembling ourselves together, that we exhort one another.

If we put all these together, the biblical fact is that we should assemble. In the scriptures, we see that the saints gathered in one place. This thought is all over the epistles and the book of Acts. It is this frequent coming together of the saints that we describe by the terminology "local church" or "local assembly", though the fact is that the terms "local assembly" or "local church" are not in the bible.

Some observations from the book of Revelation

In the book of revelation, John writes to believers:

5. And from Jesus Christ, who is the faithful witness, and the first begotten of the dead, and the prince of the kings of the earth. Unto him, that loved us, and washed us from our sins in his own blood, 6. And hath made us kings and priests unto God and his Father; to him be glory and dominion for ever and ever. Amen.
Revelation 1:5-6

John is writing to those that have been made kings and priests unto God. Jesus has loved these kings and priests by washing them from their sins in His own blood. These are the saints.

4. John to the seven churches which are in Asia: Grace be unto you, and peace, from him which is, and which was, and which is to come; and from the seven Spirits which are before his throne;
Revelation 1:4

John has written to the seven churches in Asia. Therefore, we know that it is humans that John addressed the book of revelation to.

Observe this pattern:

Unto the angel of the church of Ephesus write; (Revelation 2:1).

Unto the angel of the church of Smyrna write; (Revelation 2:8).

Unto the angel of the church of Pergamos write; (Revelation 2:12).

Unto the angel of the church of Thyatira write; (Revelation 2:18).

Unto the angel of the church of Sardis write; (Revelation 3:1).

Unto the angel of the church of Philadelphia write; (Revelation 3:7).

Unto the angel of the church of the Laodiceans write; (Revelation 3:14).

Each of the churches that John mentions has an angel. We also observe that each time John writes to a local church, he also specifically mentions the angel of that local church. It is to the angel of each church that he directs his epistle.

What does he mean by the angel of the church?

It is the same Greek word that has been translated "angel" in each instance. This Greek word is used elsewhere in other epistles.

Writing to the Galatians, Paul says:

> *14. And my temptation which was in my flesh ye despised not, nor rejected; but received me as an angel of God, even as Christ Jesus.*
> *Galatians 4:14*

The same word that has been translated "angel" in "angel of the church of" in Revelation 2 and 3, is used here, in the "angel of God." The Galatians know that Paul's "angel of God" is a reference to himself.

Paul commended the Galatians for receiving him as an angel of God. He does not mean that he is not a man but a class of angelic beings. He simply means that he came to them as one with the message of God - the gospel.

Thus, the term angel can be used for men on account of the message that they preach. Luke used the same term in describing the disciples of John:

> *24. And when the messengers of John were departed, he began to speak unto the people concerning John, What went ye out into the wilderness for to see? A reed shaken with the wind?*
> *Luke 7:24*

The word that has been translated "angel" in "angel of the church of" in Revelation 2 and 3 is the same that has been translated as "messengers" in "the messengers of John." Luke called those disciples of John that John had sent to Jesus the messengers or angels of John. They were John's envoy. Since they had come with John's message, they were John's angels. Luke also used this term in describing the disciples of Jesus:

51. And it came to pass, when the time was come that he should be received up, he stedfastly set his face to go to Jerusalem, 52. And sent messengers before his face: and they went, and entered into a village of the Samaritans, to make ready for him.
Luke 9:51-52

Again, the same word used for "angel" in "angel of the church of" in Revelation 2 and 3 has been translated as "messengers" in "sent messengers before his face". Luke referred to those disciples of Jesus that He had sent ahead of Him to Samaria, the messengers or angels of Jesus. Jesus also used this same word to describe the ministry of John the Baptist:

10. For this is he, of whom it is written, Lo! I send mine angel before thy face, that shall make ready thy way before thee [which shall make ready thy way before thee].
Matthew 11:10 (WYCLIFFE)

John the Baptist was the angel that prepared Israel to receive Jesus' ministry. Thus, the term angel can also be used for men.

Therefore, when John writes to the angel of each of the seven churches, he is using parabolic language to refer to those men who bring the word of God to each of those churches. The angel of each of those churches would be the pastor exercising ministerial oversight over each of those 7 churches mentioned in Revelation 2 and 3.

Since there was no church that John wrote to without writing to the angel of that church, we can affirm that the things John had to say to each local church, he said to the angel of that assembly.

We can also affirm that there is no local church if there is no angel of that local church. The local church must have those exercising ministerial oversight. Therefore, the local church is not merely the coming together of saints in one place, for the assembly to be the local church;

it also has the distinction of having an angel set over its affairs.

Does the local assembly need to have an angel (men exercising ministerial oversight) whenever the saints come together? Yes, they do.

Do the saints need to have an angel (men exercising ministerial oversight) present whenever they come together? No, they do not.

The difference in the two answers above is that not every gathering together of saints is a local church.

If we use John's terminology in the book of Revelation, the scriptural pattern is for each local church to have its own angel. This shows that although all the saints have been cleansed by the same blood, and built into one church in the act of Jesus' resurrection, each local church is distinct in its location, angel (or ministerial oversight), and the saints that assemble there. The one thing that distinguishes one local assembly from another would be the angels of those churches. The angel (pastor) of each local church is distinct.

19. As many as I love, I rebuke and chasten: be zealous therefore, and repent.
Revelation 3:19

The letter that John sent to each church was the Lord's rebuke of that local church. Each letter was directed to the angel of that church. The angel (minister) would then be expected to instruct the saints in each of the local churches in line with the apostolic rebuke.

Through the writings of John in the book of revelation, we observe that though there were individual saints in each of the seven churches that John had written to, there were no personal rebukes in the book of revelation. Not one of the rebukes to the seven churches were to individuals. Rather, it is within the community of saints in the local church that the believer renews the mind and learns to reason scripturally by learning to give the word first-place.

It is instructive that in John's letter, the Lord Jesus addresses believers from the perspective of the local assembly. The repentance that the

Lord Jesus speaks of in the book of Revelation is the change in the slant of the local church. There is a way each local church reasons.

Since both the Lord Jesus and John saw the saints' repentance as a local church thing, the saint best renews the mind, walks in the spirit, and learns doctrine with other saints in the local assembly.

Now, we observe that the rebukes in the book of Revelation came via angels in each of the local churches. The rebuking of the local church is the responsibility of the angel of that local assembly and not just anyone.

Here's Luke comment concerning these angels in the churches:

21. And when they had preached the gospel to that city, and had taught many, they returned again to Lystra, and to Iconium, and Antioch, 22. Confirming the souls of the disciples, and exhorting them to continue in the faith, and that we must through much tribulation enter into the kingdom of God. 23. And when they had ordained them elders in every church, and had prayed with fasting, they commended them to the Lord, on whom they believed.
Acts 14:21-23

As a result of Barnabas and Paul's ministry, the gospel was preached, people were taught, and elders were ordained in every city. These elders were not exercising oversight over the city but over the local assemblies.

Luke is emphatic that Barnabas and Paul "ordained them elders in every church". This was their practice. It is the same idea that John refers to as the angel of the church, that Luke refers to as "elder".

See what Paul told Titus concerning these "angels" in the churches:

5. For this cause left I thee in Crete, that thou shouldest set in order the things that are wanting, and ordain elders in every city, as I had appointed thee:
Titus 1:5

Paul's instruction to Titus is instructive.

The Greek word "and" between the expressions "thou shouldest set in order the things that are wanting" and "ordain elders in every city" is kai, a word that could be further describing another word or at other times a word joining two distinct ideas. In this case, the ordination of elders is the setting in order the things that are wanting in the churches.

Since Titus was to ordain elders in every city, then every local church must have its own elders.

This confirms that without the elders or angels of the churches, we'll have dysfunctional churches. It would be unscriptural. Titus was to ensure that all the local churches had elders. Paul could not conceive of local churches without elders. Even John too did not write to a local church without elders.

Thus, we see that Paul and Barnabas ordained the elders in every church and that Paul instructed Titus to do the same.

Combining the teaching of John and the practice of Barnabas and Paul, we can say that if it is the local church, it'll have an angel or elder over the assembly. We do not refer to a gathering as a local church if it has no elders or angels of that local church.

Who are elders?

Elders ordained in every church

5. For this cause left I thee in Crete, that thou shouldest set in order the things that are wanting, and ordain elders in every city, as I had appointed thee: 6. If any be blameless, the husband of one wife, having faithful children not accused of riot or unruly. 7. For a bishop must be blameless, as the steward of God; not selfwilled, not soon angry, not given to wine, no striker, not given to filthy lucre;
Titus 1:5-7

In his introduction, after he affirms that he is writing to Titus, Paul does not take long before letting Titus know the pressing need regarding elders. Similarly, Paul left Titus in Crete so Titus might appoint elders.

Thus, elders are not ordained in the universal church but in the local church. There are no universal elders alive today. All the elders are in relation to the local church. The sphere of the elder's operation is in the local church.

As he hath been taught

9. Holding fast the faithful word as he hath been taught, that he may be able by sound doctrine both to exhort and to convince the gainsayers.
Titus 1:9

The elder does not emerge from thin air. Rather, he must have been taught sound doctrine even grounded in it. His key role is to hold fast to the faithful word as he has been taught. Paul's practice was to ordain elders in every church (see Acts 14:23). It was in the local church that elders are identified and ordained. Not in the universal church. Each local church was to have its own elders.

In Acts 14:24, "when they had ordained them elders" is one Greek word, which Robert Young, says means "to elect by stretching out the hand." Thus, this ordination is a definite act.

Does a disciple automatically function as an elder by meeting those qualifications that have been set out in the scriptures? While it is obvious that it is the disciples that become elders, Luke shows that elders are ordained. The word translated ordain means "to elect by stretching out the hand." A distinct act. So, a disciple does not automatically function as an elder in the local church.

Paul also instructed Titus to "ordain elders in every city, as I had appointed thee." So, it was not only Paul that ordained elders. People like Titus also ordained elders. Paul even gave both Titus and Timothy the qualifications to watch out for in elders (see 1 Timothy 3). Therefore, eldership is not mysterious, because we know what to look out for. Thus, the ordination of elders is valid today.

While giving instructions about the ordination of elders, Paul interchanged elder with another term "bishop." By referring to these elders as bishops, he shows that the terms elders and bishops can be switched.

The elder is a steward of God. A steward manages the wealth or estate of another. In this case, the elder manages the saints as the wealth of God. The elder is also a steward of sound doctrine.

The elder is not self-willed. He understands that the message and the people are God's and he or she embraces the will of God and prioritizes it over all else.

It was as High Priest, an elder in Israel, that Ananias, commanded them that stood by him to smite Paul on the mouth (see Acts 23:2)! Religious thinking makes an elder unleash violence against those with whom he disagrees,

The bishop must be blameless. Paul repeats this in Titus 1:6 and v7. It is an emphasis not to be glossed over. Firstly, being blameless is the gift of salvation (see 1 Corinthians 1:8). Thus, these elders must be saints. Being blameless is explained in the words that follow it in Titus 1:6-7. It means the elder must meet the qualifications stated regarding sound conduct and in faithful commitment to sound doctrine.

> *21. And when they had preached the gospel to that city, and had taught many, they returned again to Lystra, and to Iconium, and Antioch, 22. Confirming the souls of the disciples, and exhorting them to continue in the faith, and that we must through much tribulation enter into the kingdom of God. 23. And when they had ordained them elders in every church, and had prayed with fasting, they commended them to the Lord, on whom they believed. 24. And after they had passed throughout Pisidia, they came to Pamphylia.*
>
> *Act 14:21-24*

Observe the sequence:

First, Paul confirmed the souls of the disciples and exhorted them to continue in the faith. This continuing in the faith is by continuing in the word of God. It is submission to the word.

Afterward, he ordained elders.

Lastly, he left those ordained elders who remained in those churches, while he moved on to do ministry elsewhere.

The implication is that these elders are needed in his absence, to carry out the work that they had watched Paul faithfully discharge towards the disciples in their presence. The elders would be the ones to continue with the task of "confirming the souls of the disciples, and exhorting them to continue in the faith".

Thus, elders exist to see to it that the word of God is obeyed.

Once Paul moved on from each church, the elders that he had ordained remain in each church. He was the elder while he was there amongst them, for the shepherd needs to be with the sheep. He had trained the disciples and ordained elders who he commended to the Lord. These elders exercise oversight over each of those assemblies.

Again, here's what Paul told Titus:

> *5. For this cause left I thee in Crete, that thou shouldest set in order the things that are wanting, and ordain elders in every city, as I had appointed thee: 6. If any be blameless, the husband of one wife, having faithful children not accused of riot or unruly. 7. For a bishop must be blameless, as the steward of God; not selfwilled, not soon angry, not given to wine, no striker, not given to filthy lucre;*
> *Titus 1:5-7*

Paul had been in Crete. Then he left Titus there. Paul's "For this cause left I thee in Crete, that thou" means that once Paul left Titus in Crete, Titus was the elder in Crete. Titus was the one who could then set things in order. Paul was no longer the elder over Crete. To exercise proper eldership, he would need to be in Crete with the people and setting things in order in their midst.

At inception, new assemblies need ordained elders to exercise oversight. These elders need to be with the congregation, otherwise, they are elders only in name but not in reality.

Paul's "ordain elders in every city" means that elders are ordained by men who observe them. it is not up to God who will or who will not be an elder.

It was the practice of the apostles to tell the saints to "look ye out among you seven men of honest report, full of the Holy Ghost and wisdom, whom we may appoint over this business" (see Acts 6:3). Thus, although the apostles did the appointing, it was the saints that had previously made the selection of those whom the apostles would later appoint. It was the apostles that set the criteria. However, it was the saints who had looked out among themselves to select the men. Titus would have these facts at the back of his mind as he appoints or ordains the elders in each local church.

The elders do not act for the assembly in selecting new elders.

The saints do not do the ordaining or appointing.

Today, it'll also be our practice to stay apostolic by letting the saints do the selection, while the elders appoint the new elders.

Elders are overseers that feed

5. The reason I left you in Crete was that you might put in order what was left unfinished and appoint elders in every town, as I directed you.
Titus 1:5 (NIV)

Titus was to ordain elders in every local church. Each church was to have its own elders.

7. For a bishop must be blameless, as the steward of God; not selfwilled, not soon angry, not given to wine, no striker, not given to filthy lucre;
Titus 1:7

In describing the qualifications of the elders, Paul referred to them as bishops or overseers. Thus, elders and bishops are interchangeable words. The terms elders, bishops, and overseers are one and the same.

17. And from Miletus he sent to Ephesus, and called the elders of the church.
Acts 20:17

These are the elders of the church at Ephesus, and not that of Antioch, Jerusalem, or elsewhere. It is most definitely not the universal church. This is the local church.

The term "elders of" identifies the elders with the local church.

28. Keep watch over yourselves and all the flock of which the Holy Spirit has made you overseers. Be shepherds of the church of God, which he bought with his own blood.
Acts 20:28 (NIV)

Paul is clear that God has made a provision of oversight in the local church. He then teaches "the Holy Ghost has made you overseers." Thus, the Holy Ghost has made the elders in each local assembly the overseers of that local assembly.

The role of overseer is not something that one is born with. Paul does not also say that the Holy Ghost hath made every saint overseers of the local church.

The oversight of the local church is not from some far-away planet. It is by the elders who are also local.

Those who had been identified as elders in Acts 20:17, he now refers to as overseers who are shepherds that feed the church of God. This church of God is the local church where the elders are found. The universal church has no need of being fed. The word translated overseer means bishops. Where the KJV says "feed the church," the NIV correctly translates as "Be shepherds of the church." The word translated "feed" means to pastor.

So, elders take the oversight of feeding the congregation the word of God.

Who were these elders to oversee? They were to oversee "all the flock"

Recall that these elders were from Ephesus. Therefore, "all the flock" means the saints in their Ephesian churches.

The Holy Ghost had not made these Ephesian elders overseers over the Jerusalem churches. This is an important point not to be overlooked.

Here's what Peter said about oversight:

1. So as your fellow elder and a witness of Christ's sufferings and as one who shares in the glory that will be revealed, I urge the elders among you: 2 Give a shepherd's care to God's flock among you, exercising oversight not merely as a duty but willingly under God's direction, not for shameful profit but eagerly
1 Peter 5:1-2 (NET)

Peter is clear that God has made a provision of oversight in the local church. The oversight of the churches is a gift of Christ. The word translated oversight is episkopeo. It is used only in Heb 12:15 and here. It means a watchman upon, one who observes or examines the situation of the sheep. One who looks after or inspects.

Peter shows that it is the elders that are to take the oversight as shepherds.

When teaching the elders to take oversight, he said, "God's flock among you." Thus, the oversight is God's gift of a shepherd's care through men. "Among you" defines the scope of oversight. The scope of the oversight is not over every saint in every place or over saints dead or alive. It is over the saints "among you". Therefore, it is not a universal oversight.

The implication is that the oversight of an elder is not remote. The elder is with the saints that he or she pastors. An elder of the local church will be with the local church, otherwise, that elder does not have the oversight.

The elders do not exercise oversight over one who is not a saint, for the scope of the oversight is "the flock of God."

The chief reason for elders is to exercise oversight.

What does this oversight mean?

2 to be compassionate shepherds who tenderly care for God's flock and who feed them well, for you have the responsibility to guide, protect, and oversee. Consider it a joyous pleasure and not merely a religious duty. Lead from the heart under God's leadership—not as a way to gain finances dishonestly but as a way to eagerly and cheerfully serve. 3 Don't be controlling tyrants but lead others by your beautiful examples to the flock
1 Peter 5:2-3 (TPT)

Since Peter commands the elders to take the oversight, it means that it is not every saint that oversees. He said, "be compassionate shepherds who tenderly care for God's flock and who feed them well, for you have the responsibility to guide, protect, and oversee" (see 1 Peter 5:2). The feeding that guides, protects, and oversees is the oversight.

Taking the oversight means that elders are to see to it that the saints are taught sound doctrine.

3. Neither as being lords over God's heritage, but being ensamples to the flock.
1 Peter 5:3

Oversight is the God-given responsibility to show "your beautiful examples" to the flock of God. Peter is clear that oversight does not imply lordship on the part of the elders.

Also, elders are not to be as lords or controlling tyrants over God's heritage. Thus, oversight and lordship are different. Peter's choice of words shows that the opposite of showing an example is the exhibition of lordship. This means that elders go about their role in the spirit of service.

The elder takes the oversight by being solid examples of sound doctrine in their own conduct. We observe that an elder is not merely someone who is able to teach God's word. The elder must be available to the flock to serve them by setting scriptural examples for them to follow. Therefore, elders are the chief ensamples to the flock. They best watch our conduct in sound doctrine by watching theirs and seeing to it that it models the spirit of Christ.

Peter's charge is a sobering one. He shows that there are saints who can teach but who also want to lord it over those saints that they teach in the local church. Such saints do not pay attention to the fact that oversight demands that they be expressions of godly examples. Such men and women are worldly and are not given to a heart of service although they can talk a good talk.

Those who are elders and are running afoul of Peter's charge are to repent.

The role of the elder is God's gift to the local church. It is God's idea. The dangerous mindset that says, "I will do my thing my way" is not God's trait in the elders. The local church is not man's way but God's. Also, the flock is not the elders' but God's.

Peter continues:

4. And when the chief Shepherd shall appear, ye shall receive a crown of glory
that fadeth not away.
1 Peter 5:4

Jesus is the chief of the shepherds. The elders are under-shepherds under Him.

What does Peter mean by "ye shall receive a crown of glory that fadeth not away"?

He means that Jesus will reward on account of the way the elder has treated the flock of the chief shepherd of the sheep. The Lord comes with His reward for those who have faithfully discharged the work of an elder.

Elders are men and women that can hold you to the light that you have and to see to it that you do not walk beneath that light possessed.

The qualities that Peter anticipates in elders are: (a) they know they serve God's flock, not their own, (b) they lovingly guide and care for God's flock, (c) they take the duties of oversight willingly, (d) they are driven by service, and not financial gain, (e) they feed and tend God's people, (f) they shun a domineering slant, (g) they lead by setting beautiful examples.

17. The elders who direct the affairs of the church well are worthy of double
honor, especially those whose work is preaching and teaching
1 Timothy 5:17 (NIV)

All elders direct the affairs of the church, amongst them there are those elders that rule by labouring in the word and doctrine. They feed the saints by preaching and teaching the word.

> *22. Then pleased it the apostles and elders, with the whole church, to send chosen men of their own company to Antioch with Paul and Barnabas; namely, Judas surnamed Barsabas, and Silas, chief men among the brethren:*
> *Acts 15:22*

We find that the apostles and elders are with the whole church. This "whole church" was the church at Jerusalem and not the church at Ephesus or Antioch. These apostles and elders are not operative in the universal church.

The company of Apostles and elders sent two men, Judas and Silas to Antioch with Paul and Barnabas. These men would be classed together with the apostles or with the elders. Since it is usually the twelve that are referred to as apostles at the Jerusalem church, Judas and Silas would be elders.

As elders, Judas and Silas are referred to as "chief men" amongst the brethren. The term means leader. It refers to those who rule or have oversight "among the brethren."

> *27. We have sent therefore Judas and Silas, who shall also tell you the same things by mouth.*
> *Acts 15:27*

The elders, Judas and Silas, would exercise oversight by saying what the apostles would have said had they travelled to Antioch from Jerusalem. Thus, Judas and Silas are elders who address the local assembly. They taught the apostles' epistles to the saints at Antioch (verse 30).

This epistle settled a doctrinal dispute (Acts 15:1-2).

> *32. And Judas and Silas, being prophets also themselves, exhorted the brethren with many words, and confirmed them.*
> *Acts 15:32*

Judas and Silas were prophets whose ministry in the local church was to teach, exhort, and confirm the saints.

> *22. Then the apostles and elders, with the whole church, decided to choose some of their own men and send them to Antioch with Paul and Barnabas. They chose Judas (called Barsabbas) and Silas, men who were leaders among the believers.*
> *Acts 15:22 (NIV)*

These prophets, Judas and Silas "were leaders among the believers." They had been classed together with the elders in the Jerusalem meeting.

Antioch and Jerusalem

> *1. And certain men which came down from Judaea taught the brethren, and said, Except ye be circumcised after the manner of Moses, ye cannot be saved.*
> *Acts 15:1*

These "certain men" that came to Antioch were not members of the local church at Antioch. They taught "Except ye be circumcised after the manner of Moses, ye cannot be saved". These "certain" men were "of the sect of the Pharisees which believed" (see Acts 15:5).

> *2. This brought Paul and Barnabas into sharp dispute and debate with them. So Paul and Barnabas were appointed, along with some other believers, to go up to Jerusalem to see the apostles and elders about this question.*
> *Acts 15:2 (NIV)*

Paul and Barnabas were elders at the Antioch church. They knew that what these saints (teachers) from the Jerusalem church were teaching was false and needed correction. However, the saints from Jerusalem did not receive correction from Paul and Barnabas concerning their false doctrine. They decided instead to go to Jerusalem instead, where the elders of the Jerusalem church were.

Paul and Barnabas went "along with some other believers" from the Antioch church.

The spokesman of the "sect of the Pharisees which believed" spoke (Acts 15:5).

After that, the apostles and elders came together to consider the matter (Acts 15:6).

After the apostles and elders had disputed the matter, Peter spoke as the spokesman of the apostles (Acts 15:7).

Then, lastly, James as the spokesman of the elders spoke (Acts 15:5).

Consider what James said:

24 Since we have heard that some have gone out from among us with no orders from us and have confused you, upsetting your minds by what they said,
Acts 15:24 (NET)

James, the spokesman for the elders at Jerusalem, acknowledged that it was saints from the Jerusalem church that had caused the trouble in the Antioch church. Their teachings confused and upset the minds of the saints. The teaching of these teachers from the "sect of the Pharisees which believed" moved the saints away from assurance in Christ.

James corrected the "some" that "have gone out from among us", and was emphatic that their false teaching had troubled the saints and subverted their souls. He publicly administered the correction, saying the men had taught "with no orders from us." Thus, emphasising that the teaching of these "some" from the Jerusalem church was contrary to what James and the other elders taught in the Jerusalem church.

27. We have sent therefore Judas and Silas, who shall also tell you the same things by mouth.
Acts 15:27

It was the elders at Jerusalem that sent Judas and Silas to the church at Antioch. These men would communicate the correction of the "some" which had come from Jerusalem church to the Antioch church. By this correction, they'll publicly affirm that Paul and Barnabas had been right to have opposed their teaching by the sharp dispute and debate that they had with the "some" from Jerusalem.

Observe that it was not Paul and Barnabas that sent Judas and Silas to the church at Antioch. Only James could do that. James was their pastor, neither Paul nor Barnabas were.

There were men asides Paul and Barnabas, who could confirm that James and the elders at Jerusalem corrected those saints who had come to trouble the saints at Antioch.

Also, observe that James sent a letter to emphatically confirm that the saints over whom he exercised oversight, and who had come to Antioch, had been wrong in their teaching.

Paul did not relocate to the Jerusalem church as a result, nor did he assume eldership over the saints there to assume the teaching function in the Jerusalem church. That was James' responsibility.

More importantly, we observe that James did not head over to the Antioch church. He stayed in the local church at Jerusalem where he was a spokesman for the elders. Jerusalem was where his oversight was strong and not Antioch. Whatever needed to be sorted at Antioch, Paul and Barnabas were to see to that as elders over the church at Antioch.

As students of the scriptures, we must not rush over these points that Luke brings to our attention.

Peter, the apostle, is an elder

1. To the elders among you, I appeal as a fellow elder and a witness of Christ's sufferings who also will share in the glory to be revealed: 2. Be shepherds of God's flock that is under your care, watching over them—not because you must, but because you are willing, as God wants you to be; not pursuing dishonest gain, but eager to serve;
1 Peter 5:1-2 (NIV)

Peter referred to himself as a fellow elder. By this, we know that an Apostle is an elder whereas it is not necessarily true that an elder is an apostle.

Peter is also instructing the elders. Since Peter spoke to "the elders among you", it means that the elders are found amongst the saints.

The term "among you" is a reference to the gathering in the local church. Peter is not addressing the universal church in the Epistles. Since the elders are among you in the local church, we see that the sphere of the elder's operation is in the local church.

Peter's instruction to the elders to "be shepherds of God's flock that is under your care" is from what Jesus had told Peter "feed my sheep" (see John 21:15). Thus, the instruction to feed or shepherd the flock was not only to Peter. Other elders feed (pastor or shepherd) the flock.

Elders gather the church

Since Peter, who is one of the twelve apostles, identifies himself as an elder, we know that the twelve apostles were elders.

2. Then the twelve called the multitude of the disciples unto them, and said, It is not reason that we should leave the word of God, and serve tables.
Acts 6:2

The twelve apostles "called the multitude of the disciples unto them" means that it was the elders that called the meetings of the local assembly. The local assembly is not just the gathering of saints, but the assembly called by the elders.

The assembly in the universal church is Christ's work in the resurrection. It is referred to as God's call (2 Tim 1:9;1 Thess 4:7;1 Cor 1:9,26;7:22, Rom 9:24). It is not a call by elders or any man.

The local church is called or assembled by the elders.

Here's what was said about Barnabas and Paul:

> *27. And when they were come, and had gathered the church together, they rehearsed all that God had done with them, and how he had opened the door of faith unto the Gentiles.*
> *Acts 14:27*

It is the elders that gather the saints together in the local church.

Hear Paul:

> *7. As ye also learned of Epaphras our dear fellowservant, who is for you a faithful minister of Christ;*
> *Colossians 1:7*

The church at Colosse gathered to receive the oversight of Epaphras. Paul did not need to be there in order for them to be a valid assembly. It was enough that "Epaphras our dear fellow servant" was a faithful minister of Christ to them.

Paul traced their knowledge of Christ to Epaphras, for he said, "Ye also learned of Epaphras." This means that the saints had been taught by Epaphras, who was the elder exercising oversight in Colosse.

Elder is a generic term

We note that Peter, an apostle, had referred to himself as an elder (see 1 Peter 5:1). Judas and Silas, who were prophets, had also been classed amongst the elders (See Acts 15:32).

23. And they wrote letters by them after this manner; The apostles and elders
and brethren send greeting unto the brethren which are of the Gentiles in
Antioch and Syria and Cilicia:
Acts 15:23

"Apostles and elders and brethren" was how they referred to everyone present at the Jerusalem meeting. All that were present were brethren. Amongst the brethren, some were elders. Among the elders, some were apostles. If you were at that meeting, and you were a minister but not one of the apostles, you were referred to as elder.

Since Peter had also referred to the apostles as elders, the term "apostles and elders" can be summarised as elders. This means that "elder" is a generic term for referring to recognised ministries amongst the saints.

11. And he gave some, apostles; and some, prophets; and some, evangelists; and
some, pastors and teachers; 12. For the perfecting of the saints, for the work of
the ministry, for the edifying of the body of Christ:
Ephesians 4:11-12

Paul's apostles, prophets, evangelists, pastors, and teachers are generically referred to as elders. Therefore, Paul is describing the elders.

The saint is complete in Christ and has been endowed with the spirit as the riches of God.

However, God gave the elders to the saints to train the saints so that God's endowment and deposits in the saints come forth.

These elders are "for the perfecting of the saints, for the work of the ministry". The term that has been translated "perfecting" means to "equip", "nurture and prepare" or to make a thing function as it should. This does not create the saint. Rather, it recognises the saint as God's work in the new creation and labours over the saint in order that the saint might function as designed. God has wired the saint for ministry. The elders see to it that the saints do the work of the ministry. This is the perfecting supplied by the elders. Technically, it does not refer to growth.

13. Till we all come in the unity of the faith, and of the knowledge of the Son of God, unto a perfect man, unto the measure of the stature of the fulness of Christ:
Ephesians 4:13

This is the effect of the elders on the saints, who are to do the work of ministry

To do the work of ministry, the saints need to have the knowledge of the Son of God, which is a clear grasp of what the Lord has accomplished in redemption.

Earlier in his letter to the Ephesians, Paul had described this as the eyes of the saint's understanding being enlightened so they might know the exceeding greatness of resurrection power. The elders open the eyes of the saints to see light through the knowledge of what the Son has done and feed the flock by continually supplying knowledge of the Son of God. This is how the elders perfect the saints for the work of ministry.

"Till we all come in the unity of the faith," describes how each saint comes in the unity of the faith. This does not describe a designated day or hour that every single member of the body of Christ has come in the unity of the faith. We receive the ministry of the elders collectively but our growth is not collective. Each saint grows individually. The more our eyes are enlightened by the ministry of the elders, the more effective the saint's work of ministry.

14. That we henceforth be no more children, tossed to and fro, and carried about with every wind of doctrine, by the sleight of men, and cunning craftiness, whereby they lie in wait to deceive;
Ephesians 4:14

If we could summarise the job description of elders, it is captured in these words - no more children. This means elders take children and make more elders. This is spiritual growth. The elders are not the only ministries. They feed the flock and by this stir the ministries in every other saint.

Thus, the effect of the oversight of the elders on the saints is that the saints mature from being children who are tossed to and fro to become "no more children".

16. From whom the whole body fitly joined together and compacted by that which every joint supplieth, according to the effectual working in the measure of every part, maketh increase of the body unto the edifying of itself in love.
Ephesians 4:16

The one body that Christ built in His resurrection is His work alone. That universal body has Christ as God's supply. This "whole body" that Paul speaks of, refers to the saints in the local assembly.

The effect of the elder on the saints is the work of ministry performed by the saint. It is the saints' work of ministry that Paul refers to as "that which every joint supplieth". The growth in the saint causes those saints who receive and respond to the oversight of the elders to be centres of supply in the local church.

Elders and Joel's prophecy

16. But this is that which was spoken by the prophet Joel; 17. And it shall come to pass in the last days, saith God, I will pour out of my Spirit upon all flesh: and your sons and your daughters shall prophesy, and your young men shall see visions, and your old men shall dream dreams: 18. And on my servants and on my handmaidens I will pour out in those days of my Spirit; and they shall prophesy:
Acts 2:16-17

Peter explained that as a result of the work of the spirit in the saints, each saint is made a centre of supply. These saints are "my servants" and "my handmaidens", ministers of God.

The elders had a role in this:

42. And they continued stedfastly in the apostles' doctrine and fellowship, and in breaking of bread, and in prayers.
Acts 2:42

The apostles were the elders who supplied the doctrine. Wherever they ministered, that was where the saints gathered to fellowship. They were training disciples.

2. Then the twelve called the multitude of the disciples unto them, and said, It is not reason that we should leave the word of God, and serve tables.
Acts 6:2

"The twelve" was a specific way of referring to the twelve apostles who were eyewitnesses to Jesus' resurrection. We see that they were the elders in the local church at Jerusalem. The expression "the twelve called the multitude of the disciples unto them" means that it is the elders who convene the local church; they gather the saints. Without the elders, there is no local church.

3. Wherefore, brethren, look ye out among you seven men of honest report, full of the Holy Ghost and wisdom, whom we may appoint over this business.
Acts 6:3

This is a glimpse of the local church at Jerusalem.

The words "look ye out among you seven men of honest report" shows us the elders' instruction to those that they had already taught the word. The trained disciples were to look out for those men in their midst, who were showing the effect of the oversight of the elders.

6. Whom they set before the apostles: and when they had prayed, they laid their hands on them.
Acts 6:6

Although there was a shortage of natural abilities, Peter and the other apostles did not think the approach should be "let us flood the place with those who are skilled at setting tables". Interestingly, of the qualifications they told the saints to watch out for, none was about talents. The saints were to look for those men in their midst already noted for ministry. This means that these seven men had served to a degree that the whole assembly had noted it. The men were people helping the apostles in the ministry of the gospel. They showed the example of serving tables. The apostles were not looking for men that would be the most skillful at the natural arrangement of tables.

The apostles laid hands to separate these seven deacons for their service in the local church. When we lay hands upon people designated for service, there is no command for or against hands upon the head. There is no requirement to lay hands upon the head. If either the ones laying hands or the one on whom hands are laid is convinced the head is preferred, so be it.

Now, the people chose seven men. Barnabas had been singled out by name prior to this as someone who operated by the apostles' doctrine (Acts 4:36). Such was the high standard that not even Barnabas qualified (see Acts 6:5).

Nothing is said about the use of oil in the book of Acts or the epistles for ordination.

Although the apostles prayed, the seven deacons were not selected by prayer. They were selected by the people acting on the elders' instruction. The apostles prayed and then laid hands to separate those who had distinguished themselves in service.

We know that the seven would be men given to ministry, on account of the impact of their ordination on the assembly. Luke does not once record their serving tables.

7. And the word of God increased; and the number of the disciples multiplied in Jerusalem greatly; and a great company of the priests were obedient to the faith.
8. And Stephen, full of faith and power, did great wonders and miracles among the people.
Acts 6:7-8

The word translated "increased" in "the word of God increased" refers to a multitude of people. Thus, "the word of God increased" means that more people got involved in the preaching of reconciliation. When more people in the local church get involved in preaching what the Lord has done, that is the word increasing.

Therefore, we see that the oversight of the elders led to more elders emerging from those who had submitted to training by the elders. It was as a result of an increase of such elders that at least seven more people in the local church at Jerusalem got involved in preaching what the Lord had done. This was how "the word of God increased". Technically, these seven men were called deacons. Deacons are elders-in-training.

Interestingly, from this point onwards in the book of Acts, the doctrine was no longer referred to as "the apostle's doctrine". The term "apostles' doctrine" showed that initially, the apostles were the only ones teaching in the local assembly. Once "the word of God increased", the term "the apostles' doctrine" was no longer used. The elders, who were the only teachers, had produced other teachers like Stephen.

As the elders, the effect of the ministry of the apostles was that they had triggered the fulfilment of Joel's prophecy in other saints. Thus, Stephen had become one of those speaking the gospel and demonstrating its power with great wonders and miracles.

Here is something about elders and the church:

1. Paul and Timotheus, the servants of Jesus Christ, to all the saints in Christ Jesus which are at Philippi, with the bishops and deacons:
Philippians 1:1

In Paul's opening statement to the letter to the Philippians, he greets the saints in Christ, with the bishops and deacons.

The word translated "with" in "with the bishops and deacons" is the

Greek word "sun," which is used here in its associative sense. There-fore, the word means "in association with" or "together with". All that Paul says, he says to the holy ones and the leaders amongst them.

Paul does not say the saints, the bishops and the deacons. The two nouns for "bishops" and "deacons" do not have the definite article, which implies that these are not a separate group from the saints.

So, Paul is writing to the saints, showing that some of these saints are bishops and deacons. However, they are all saints. In the local church, asides the bishops and deacons amongst the saints, Paul does not rec-ognise any other distinction of groups.

The bishop is an elder, while the deacon is an elder-in-waiting or sup-porting elder. Thus, Paul greets the saints in the local church and ad-ditionally singles out the elders among them. The thing he used to distinguish amongst those saints was their work in the Lord.

Interestingly, Paul does not directly use the word "elder" in his greet-ing of the Philippians. Elder generally speaks of maturity, while over-seer or bishop describes the work of ministry.

This is the clearest greeting of the local church in the epistles. In it, we see that if what we are talking about is the local church, it will not be without its elders, who are also local.

Feed My Sheep

Sheep having no shepherd

36. But when he saw the multitudes, he was moved with compassion on them, because they fainted, and were scattered abroad, as sheep having no shepherd.
Matthew 9:36

The one great need that Jesus identified was that men were "scattered abroad, as sheep having no shepherd."

How did He tackle this?

20. Now the God of peace, that brought again from the dead our Lord Jesus, that great shepherd of the sheep, through the blood of the everlasting covenant,
Hebrews 13:20

It was as the great shepherd that Jesus assembled the church in His resurrection. Jesus is THE Shepherd or Pastor in the resurrection.

1. The LORD is my shepherd; I shall not want.
Psalm 23:1

The Lord is THE Shepherd in the resurrection.

4. And when the chief Shepherd shall appear, ye shall receive a crown of glory that fadeth not away.
1 Peter 5:4

Jesus has met the great need of man. As the firstborn from the dead, He is the chief Shepherd. We are no more sheep without a shepherd.

2. Until the day in which he was taken up, after that he through the Holy Ghost had given commandments unto the apostles whom he had chosen: 4. And, being assembled together with them, commanded them that they should not depart from Jerusalem, but wait for the promise of the Father, which, saith he, ye have heard of me.
Acts 1:2,4

Jesus was also the first Pastor of the first local church. He did not do this remotely but in person, but He "assembled together with them". Then He taught the disciples and gave instructions.

Here's what He did before the day of Pentecost:

16. He saith to him again the second time, Simon, son of Jonas, lovest thou me? He saith unto him, Yea, Lord; thou knowest that I love thee. He saith unto him, Feed my sheep.
John 21:16

Post-resurrection, Jesus, the Shepherd, commanded Peter "Feed my sheep".

In verses 15 and 17, the Greek word translated "feed" is bosko. In verse 26, a different Greek word, poimaino is used. Poimaino means to tend the flock, to shepherd, which is the same thing as pastor.

Peter knew that Jesus is the Pastor. When Jesus commanded Peter to feed (pastor) Jesus' sheep, Peter and the other apostles understood that Jesus, the pastor, would exercise His post-resurrection service (Pastor) through men, who are called pastors. Jesus was giving Himself to the flock through men like Peter who would tend the flock as Shepherds and not as Generals. Why did Jesus do this?

Seeing His labour expressed

38. Pray ye therefore the Lord of the harvest, that he will send forth labourers into his harvest.
Matthew 9:38

As the Lord of the harvest, Jesus would send forth or release Himself in the labour of these men that He identified as "labourers".

Therefore, when these saints saw the same work of pastor that they had seen Jesus demonstrate now become pronounced in Peter, they understood that Peter was letting Jesus work through him. Jesus is the pastor in the resurrection. He is the gift of ministry. He acted through Peter's yielding.

The others saw Peter, the shepherd, and they knew that behind the scenes, the great Shepherd was being given expression.

16. He saith to him again the second time, Simon, son of Jonas, lovest thou me?
He saith unto him, Yea, Lord; thou knowest that I love thee. He saith unto him,
Feed my sheep.
John 21:16

The sheep in "feed my sheep" were the other apostles and disciples of Jesus that were present. Jesus wants His flock fed and the feeding of the flock is by someone amongst them. Jesus would serve through Peter, the same labour that Peter had observed in Jesus as the Shepherd over His flock. The key difference was that whereas, Jesus could refer to the flock as "My sheep", Peter could not do the same, for it is Jesus alone that is "the Shepherd and Bishop of your souls". In any case, there can be no local assembly if there is no elder.

Jesus' instruction to Peter to "feed My sheep" was His instruction to the other apostles but Peter had a higher responsibility. Interestingly, all these men that Jesus referred to as sheep had been trained by the same teacher – Jesus. They had listened to the same profound explanations. Yet, Jesus appointed Peter to tend them all.

He said to him (Peter), "Feed my lambs" (John 21:15).

Then He said unto him, Feed my "sheep" (John 21:16).

Again, Jesus said unto him, "Feed my sheep" (John 21:17).

Jesus' emphasis on the feeding of His flock shows that the oversight supplied via elders is extremely important to the saints. The saint will grow best by being fed by other saints who act as elders through whom the saint will learn doctrine.

Some of these others who Jesus tells Peter to feed are the very highest class of Apostles – those who were eyewitnesses to His resurrection. Yet, by the nature of the assignment that Jesus gave to Peter, we know that even they needed the oversight of Peter.

Every saint operates better when fed by elders.

It is on account of the sacredness of the feeding of the flock in the local assembly, that Jesus appointed Peter an elder. Jesus would use Peter's labour to bring about the spiritual growth of the flock of Jesus.

Peter exercised oversight in the selection of other elders:

> *21. Wherefore of these men which have companied with us all the time that the Lord Jesus went in and out among us, 22. Beginning from the baptism of John, unto that same day that he was taken up from us, must one be ordained to be a witness with us of his resurrection. 23. And they appointed two, Joseph called Barsabas, who was surnamed Justus, and Matthias.*
> *Acts 1:21-23*

In this meeting, Peter was the one who stood up among the disciples (verse 15). Peter was fulfilling the grave task Jesus had set for him to exercise oversight. The others expected him to, because they had been well taught by Jesus to receive from Peter.

Peter explained that the twelve had been ordained to be witnesses of Jesus' resurrection. He also explained the qualifications of the initial apostles and the replacement that they were about to select. It had to be someone who went in and out among the other disciples "from the baptism of John, unto that same day that he was taken up from us". No one can meet this qualification today. Even now, we observe that qualifications for choosing elders are never shrouded in mystery.

Peter based his instructions on the scriptures.

20. For it is written in the book of Psalms, Let his habitation be desolate, and let no man dwell therein: and his bishoprick let another take.
Acts 1:20

Peter taught that Judas' apostleship was a bishopric. Thus, apostles are bishops or overseers. Therefore, they are elders.

Since these elders are men who stayed faithful "from the baptism of John, unto that same day that he was taken up from us", Peter showed that asides their grasp of sound doctrine, the chief qualifications of these elders were consistency and faithfulness. It was not just their knowledge of sound doctrine.

It is not improbable that some of the men who had not been appointed as elders had a clearer understanding than some of the apostles. Although knowledge of the word is critical, knowledge in and of itself is not the characteristic that marks out elders. There is a solidity in consistency and faithfulness that is required in the elders. Some think the elder's role stop as the preaching of good and impeccable sermons. They do not see the need for adorning the doctrine in their conduct. However, elders ensure that the demands of the word are upheld not only in speech but in the conduct birthed by sound doctrine.

The elder gives direction to knowledge

Peter did not decide what they were to do based on a whim. He gave direction to their knowledge of scripture. He could show what they were to do from scripture.

14. But Peter, standing up with the eleven, lifted up his voice, and said unto them, Ye men of Judaea, and all ye that dwell at Jerusalem, be this known unto you, and hearken to my words: 15. For these are not drunken, as ye suppose, seeing it is but the third hour of the day. 16. But this is that which was spoken by the prophet Joel;

Acts 2:14-16

Peter was supported by eleven other apostles, who recognized he was the presiding elder.

Peter stood up to respond to the confusion in the world on the day of Pentecost. It is likely that any of the other eleven could have preached as Peter had preached on that day. In engaging others outside that Jerusalem church, Peter was the spokesman for the group.

He said, "this is that which was spoken by the prophet Joel". He had a good grasp of scriptures, which he used to interpret and explain what was going on.

1. Now Peter and John went up together into the temple at the hour of prayer, being the ninth hour.

Acts 3:1

Jesus' inner circle was Peter, James, and John. Here we find Peter and John, two mighty pillars of the church, who were on the way to pray. Peter and John were likely alike in knowledge. However, both did not speak at the same time.

4. And Peter, fastening his eyes upon him with John, said, Look on us.

Acts 3:4

It was Peter who reached out to speak. Peter said, "Look on us". "Peter, fastening his eyes upon him with John" – Peter and John ministered to the man. Peter took the lead. He gave direction to what they both knew to do.

12. And when Peter saw it, he answered unto the people, Ye men of Israel, why marvel ye at this? or why look ye so earnestly on us, as though by our own power or holiness we had made this man to walk?
Acts 3:12

Again, we see that it was Peter who answered the people. John knew what Peter was saying. Observe also that Peter kept speaking of "us" and "our."

"Why look ye so earnestly on us"

"As though by our own power"

"We had made this man to walk"

There is much to learn from Peter, the elder, who gave expression to Jesus the Shepherd.

James recognized Peter's role

7. And when there had been much disputing, Peter rose up, and said unto them, Men and brethren, ye know how that a good while ago God made choice among us, that the Gentiles by my mouth should hear the word of the gospel, and believe.
Acts 15:7

When the church needed a big reset because they had not been ministering to the Gentiles, God orchestrated it involving Peter. Peter himself knew that God was operating through him.

1. And the apostles and brethren that were in Judaea heard that the Gentiles had also received the word of God. 2. And when Peter was come up to Jerusalem, they that were of the circumcision contended with him, 3. Saying, Thou wentest in to men uncircumcised, and didst eat with them. 4. But Peter rehearsed the matter from the beginning, and expounded it by order unto them, saying,
Acts 11:1-4

When the apostles and brethren that were in the church in Judaea heard what Peter had done, they questioned Peter.

Note that when the apostles and brethren did not understand Peter, they did not sweep it under the rug. They discussed. Though they did not initially agree with Peter, they looked forward to Peter's explanation and anticipated clarity in his words.

As a godly elder, Peter "rehearsed the matter from the beginning, and expounded it by order unto them." He explained. He did not see their question as rebellion.

> *18. When they heard these things, they held their peace, and glorified God,*
> *saying, Then hath God also to the Gentiles granted repentance unto life.*
> *Acts 11:18*

As a result of Peter's explanation, the apostles and brethren held their peace. Peter had given direction based on God's word and in his explanation, they could discern that it was God who was at work in Peter.

So, the elders' response to questions and the clarification they give to the saints make the saints understand what God is doing. A godly elder takes the questions of the church seriously.

James' clarification:

> *14. Simeon hath declared how God at the first did visit the Gentiles, to take out*
> *of them a people for his name. 15. And to this agree the words of the prophets;*
> *as it is written,*
> *Acts 15:14-15*

James confirmed that it was in the ministry of Peter that he and the other apostles and elders had discerned that God was bringing about a big re-set.

Observe that James' statements were not a PR stunt designed to massage Peter's ego. James said, "to this agree the words of the prophets;

as it is written."

James explained Amos 9:11-12 as a foundation for Peter's action.
Thus, James had examined Peter's actions in light of the written word.
He saw the scriptures in Peter's actions and through it, he discerned
the plan of God.

A good way of interpreting the plan of God is to observe the examples of scriptural, godly and sane elders.

What happens when the elders abandon their role?

Here is Paul's admonition to the elders from Ephesus:

> *28. Take heed therefore unto yourselves, and to all the flock, over the which the*
> *Holy Ghost hath made you overseers, to feed the church of God, which he hath*
> *purchased with his own blood.*
> *Acts 20:28*

God feeds His flock through His elders who He has set over His flock.
It is noteworthy that God does not directly feed the flock. He carries
out His task in and through His men whom He has tasked with the
feeding of the saints.

> *29. For I know this, that after my departing shall grievous wolves enter in among*
> *you, not sparing the flock.*
> *Acts 20:29*

Paul is insistent on the elders feeding the flock because of the reality of "grievous wolves enter in among you". He said further, "For I
know this." He wanted the elders to see it as a present danger.

"Grievous wolves enter in among you" is not referring to wild animals
let loose upon human settlements. Instead, he refers to the false teachers who are the elders that feed the flock with the wrong diet. These
false teachers are "among you."

The grave danger that the saints face is not that which prevails in the red-light district or amongst the mafias of the underworld. The danger is right within the assembly. It is the "grievous wolves who enter in among you".

> *30. Also of your own selves shall men arise, speaking perverse things, to draw*
> *away disciples after them.*
> *Acts 20:32*

Rather than continue to say "grievous wolves," Paul speaks of men that arise to draw disciples after them.

Thus, Paul's grievous wolves are men that speak in the assembly. The error starts in the local assembly. If the local assemblies were strong and scriptural, the errors would be dealt with firmly and the saints protected.

These bad elders operate by "speaking perverse things" to the flock of God. They come across as ministers also. However, they are not shepherds at heart.

> *31 Therefore be alert, remembering that night and day for three years I did not*
> *stop warning each one of you with tears. 32 And now I entrust you to God and*
> *to the message of his grace. This message is able to build you up and give you an*
> *inheritance among all those who are sanctified.*
> *Acts 20:31-32 (NET)*

To ward off these "grievous wolves", Paul reminded these elders of the word of God which Paul had rightly, doggedly and extensively taught to them over the space of three years. Given that the grievous wolves are ministers who will not spare the flock, Paul was clear that in God's plan, the elder is to protect the flock from the grievous wolves.

Notice that Paul did not say, "I know you'll have solid saints. Leave them to deal with the grievous wolves." Rather, it was the elders that he expected to do something about the grievous wolves.

This shows the foolhardiness of the saint ignoring the ministry of godly elders. Such neglect exposes the saints to the vicious attack of grievous wolves.

Since these godly elders are in the local assembly, the greatest way to hand over advantage to the grievous wolves is for the saint to stay away from the local assembly.

28. Keep watch over yourselves and all the flock of which the Holy Spirit has made you overseers. Be shepherds of the church of God, which he bought with his own blood.
Acts 20:28 (NIV)

Observe how Paul described the church of God. He called it "which he hath purchased with his own blood." It is because of God's love for the precious flock, which He purchased with His blood, that He gives elders to His flock.

The elders exist because of God's flock. The flock gathers around the elders. That is the local church.

The saints in the local assembly will either be prey for the grievous wolves or they will be un-devourable. The preservation of the flock from "grievous wolves" will be by the God-given sacred oversight of the elders.

30. Also of your own selves shall men arise, speaking perverse things, to draw away disciples after them.
Acts 20:32

30. Even some from among your very own ranks will rise up, twisting the truth to seduce people into following them instead of Jesus
Acts 20:32 (TPT)

The "grievous wolves" are men who use their ministry to draw away disciples after them. Such elders abuse their God-given oversight by pointing the flock of God at themselves. They are interested in making the saints the disciples of men rather than the disciples of Christ.

This is the chief characteristic of grievous wolves.

The local church is where the elders make the saints the disciples of Christ. The God-given role of the elder is not to make men the disciples of men but to make men the disciples of Christ, who died and rose again. Paul's warning shows that Christ does not achieve His aims amongst men apart from men. He works through men but He has not commissioned anyone to produce disciples of men.

So, the "grievous wolves" are men; the God-given protection from the "grievous wolves" are also men!

Paul's warning about the ministry of "grievous wolves" shows that it is possible to explain the scriptures, which are the story of Christ in such a way that we are speaking of men and not of Christ. In Paul's warning, we see that "grievous wolves" are men amongst us who do not spare Christ's precious flock. The scriptural answer to "grievous wolves" is solid, sound, and scriptural elders.

If the "grievous wolves" are successful in the local church, it is not because their sophistry is superior to the power of God's word. It would be because the elders have abandoned their God-given role of feeding the sheep, or the sheep disregard the warnings of the good shepherds, or a toxic combination of both. We would find that much of the epistles are written from one of these three perspectives.

The emphasis of Paul and Peter shows that the singular greatest reason why the "grievous wolves" are successful in the local church is that the elders have abandoned their God-given role of feeding the sheep. Saints that stay away from the local assembly dull their ability to discern the fleshly ministry of "grievous wolves."

The challenge in Galatia

Here is how Paul stated the challenge faced in Galatia:

6. I marvel that ye are so soon removed from him that called you into the grace

of Christ unto another gospel: 7. Which is not another; but there be some that
trouble you, and would pervert the gospel of Christ. 8. But though we, or an
angel from heaven, preach any other gospel unto you than that which we have
preached unto you, let him be accursed. 9. As we said before, so say I now again,
If any man preach any other gospel unto you than that ye have received, let him
be accursed.
Galatians 1:6-9

Paul marveled that "ye are so soon removed from him that called you
into the grace of Christ unto another gospel". How do saints move
from the grace of Christ into another? He said, "there be some that
trouble you".

How do they achieve this?

It is "if any man preach any other gospel." Therefore, it is the challenge of preaching men, the elders. It is the elders that teach the whole
assembly. What do these men do? They pervert the gospel of Christ.
Paul explains: this would come via those that "preach unto you."

He says even further, "We or an angel" could come with this perversion in doctrine, implying that the Galatians had a doctrine problem.
Doctrinal problems in the local assembly point to a problem that the
elders have. Paul implies that ministers had come to minister to the
saints in the churches of Galatia. These words were contrary to the
liberty already had in Christ.

When men came with a perversion of the gospel to Antioch, "Paul
and Barnabas had no small dissension and disputation with them."
This is because Paul and Barnabas took their God-given oversight
with all gravity.

Paul told Titus:

10. For there are many unruly and vain talkers and deceivers, specially they of
the circumcision: 11. Whose mouths must be stopped, who subvert whole houses,
teaching things which they ought not, for filthy lucre's sake.
Titus 1:10-11

These "unruly and vain talkers and deceivers" are the grievous wolves that Paul had warned against.

Paul's answers were "whose mouths must be stopped." How would these mouths be stopped? Paul said the elders "may be able by sound doctrine both to exhort and to convince the gainsayers" (see Titus 1:9).

The problem of the church at Galatia was that the elders were not exercising the oversight of opposing certain messages and stopping them from being preached in the local church. Paul's letter to the Galatians was in order that their elders might receive correction in Paul's rebuke and that these elders would then bring a re-set to the local churches of Galatia.

We do not preach ourselves

> *5. For we preach not ourselves, but Christ Jesus the Lord; and ourselves your servants for Jesus' sake.*
> *2 Corinthians 4:5*

The message of the sound elder is Christ Jesus the Lord. He is the one that God had made Lord in the resurrection from the dead (see Acts 2:36). In this message, elders let the saints know that the elders are "your servants for Jesus' sake". That means that in the local assembly, the saints are trained to receive oversight from elders, who they see as the servants of Christ. The elders serve His flock.

Again, Paul warns:

> *30. Also of your own selves shall men arise, speaking perverse things, to draw away disciples after them.*
> *Acts 20:30*

The scriptural order is for elders to let the saints know that the elders are "your servants for Jesus' sake." The elders are servants of Christ.

The grievous wolves change this order. The meaning of their message is that elders are lords and Christ is a servant. Otherwise, they would preach themselves as co-Lords with Christ. The sophisticated sort of grievous wolf will mention Christ, while really emphasizing the elders as Lords. This hurts the saints and brings a bad reputation to the local church.

Bad shepherds are the single greatest reason that the local church is rejected amongst men. Next to that would be those men that are drawn to, aid bad elders or are bad-shepherds-in-training. Afterward, we have those that shun the local church because they have an alternative to God's plan.

The answer is a return to biblical eldership that the saints can safely receive from.

The problem in Crete

10. For there are many unruly and vain talkers and deceivers, specially they of the circumcision: 11. Whose mouths must be stopped, who subvert whole houses, teaching things which they ought not, for filthy lucre's sake.
Titus 1:10-11

The church in Crete already had ministers that Paul identified as "they of the circumcision". These should have identified themselves as "they of the holy nation." They did not recognize the nation built in the resurrection but peddled the wrong doctrine. Paul did not say to pray to God that He should sort out these false preachers. Their mouths need to be stopped from preaching things that they should not have preached.

What was their motivation? Paul said they were "teaching things which they ought not, for filthy lucre's sake." They were motivated by greed - filthy lucre. The trouble with covetousness is that it is a way of reading and explaining the scriptures.

What was Paul's answer?

1. But speak thou the things which become sound doctrine:
Titus 2:1

These "things which become sound doctrine" would be spoken by the elders in the local church. Just as men are responsible for subverting whole houses, men will be responsible to combat this by speaking sound doctrine.

Rebuke sharply

5. For this cause left I thee in Crete, that thou shouldest set in order the things that are wanting, and ordain elders in every city, as I had appointed thee:
Titus 1:5

Paul had left Titus in Crete to address the need for elders in every city. These elders were needed in every city.

Elders are the God-given defence-mechanism that God has put in the local church to secure the saints against false teaching trying to creep into the lives of the saints.

What were the elders to do?

13. This witness is true. Wherefore rebuke them sharply, that they may be sound in the faith;
Titus 1:13

The elders would bring stability to the local assembly by sharply rebuking the wayward preaching of these preachers.

He repeated this charge to Timothy:

3. As I besought thee to abide still at Ephesus, when I went into Macedonia, that thou mightest charge some that they teach no other doctrine,
1 Timothy 1:3

Timothy was to charge those ministers at Ephesus who were teaching "other doctrine", in order that "they might teach no other doctrine."

In the heart of Paul, the local church is not to be a place for a variety of doctrinal views. Timothy was to make it his business to scrutinize whatever was being preached in the local assembly. The only way the body of Christ can be deceived would be for the local assembly to fail to combat unsound doctrine.

Impact of elders

10. According to the grace of God which is given unto me, as a wise masterbuilder, I have laid the foundation, and another buildeth thereon. But let every man take heed how he buildeth thereupon.
1 Corinthians 3:10

Paul had been talking about himself and Apollos as ministers.

Paul's warning was for every elder to take heed "how he buildeth thereupon."

17. If someone destroys God's temple, God will destroy him. For God's temple is holy, which is what you are.
1 Corinthians 3:17 (NET)

The temple of God is His people.

It is the ministries of the elders, which he had referred to as "let every man take heed how he buildeth thereupon", that he now describes as "if someone destroys God's temple". Thus, the ministers who destroy the temple of God do so by the things that they build thereon through the doctrines that they teach to the saints.

"Him shall God destroy" is not referring to the loss of salvation, since Paul had already said, "If any man's work shall be burned, he shall suffer loss: but he himself shall be saved; yet so as by fire" (see 1 Corinthians 3: 15). The believer is kept secure by God's power. The word "destroy" shows the severity of the matter. It refers to the consequence of destructive doctrine on the minister that perpetuates it. The testimony of such ministers will be set aside and treated as useless and unfit for the church. They forgo their reward, while God guarantees their salvation.

> *12. Now if any man build upon this foundation gold, silver, precious stones, wood, hay, stubble;*
> *1 Corinthians 3:12*

The expression "any man build upon" refers to ministry. There is quality in ministry.

There is a staggering amount that God has invested in the sacred work of the elders, such that if the proper man is not in place, much lives can be damaged because Jesus, the Shepherd, is prevented from serving His flock through mature men and women. It is Jesus' design, that by the godly oversight of the elders in the local church, the sheep are affected in a godly way.

Why the local church?

We have shown that while the term local church is not used in the scriptures, what we try to use that term to describe is. We use the term "local church" to distinguish it from the universal church, which is the one body of Christ that He built in His resurrection.

The church will not have succeeded if it competes with the world's ability to hold business seminars, host parties, carnival or act as a center for comedy and comedians. This is not because business seminars, parties, carnivals or comedy are evil; it is just not what Jesus has tasked His church with.

Suppose someone was to say, "since I belong to the one body in His resurrection, why would I need to gather with others in the local church?".

After salvation, the believer ought to be taught the fact of the local church in order that the saint awakens to ministry and spiritual growth.

23. If therefore the whole church be come together into one place, and all speak with tongues, and there come in those that are unlearned, or unbelievers, will they not say that ye are mad?
1 Corinthians 14:23

Paul speaks of "whole church" and also speaks of "one place." Therefore, this "whole church" is a reference to the whole church at Corinth.

We observe that in the local church, we have a mix of people – those who are giving expression to utterance, the unlearned and the unbelievers.

Thus, in the local assembly, all would normally be acting on the word together. The disciples are doing the same things. In this case, all speak with tongues.

"There come in those who are unlearned, unbelievers" shows that these are not disciples. Their conclusion sets them in opposition to the disciples since the unlearned and the unbelievers conclude that those saints who are speaking in tongues are mad.

Paul's instruction was not to stop the tongues. Instead, he wants us to bring understanding to the unlearned and the unbelievers. The elders are training the saints as disciples. These unlearned must also become disciples.

20. Brethren, be not children in understanding: howbeit in malice be ye children,
but in understanding be men.
1 Corinthians 14:20

The elders see to it that those who are disciples do not dumb down so that all become like "children in understanding", for in that case, the saints would think and act like the unlearned and the unbelievers. On the contrary, we raise the level of understanding and operation of the disciples so that in understanding we are men.

The disciples are actively involved in the training of the unlearned in order that we raise our level as a local assembly.

24. But if all prophesy, and there come in one that believeth not, or one
unlearned, he is convinced of all, he is judged of all:
1 Corinthians 14:24

Rather than bring the local assembly to the level of the unlearned, all the disciples have raised their game. They all prophesy. The local

Why the local Church?97

assembly is where elders train the unlearned to become disciples and
prepare the learned to be more effective disciples.

Where we know those who labour over us

*12. And we beseech you, brethren, to know them which labour among you, and
are over you in the Lord, and admonish you; 13. And to esteem them very highly
in love for their work's sake. And be at peace among yourselves.*
1 Thessalonians 5:12-13

Notice that there is a training to "know them which labour among
you." These labourers are among us. They are over us in the Lord.

The local church is where we know them which labour among you. It
is where we are admonished by them who "are over you in the Lord,
and admonish you". Those who are over us are the ones whose instructions we follow. It is in following those instructions that we grow.

Can the saint get information without being part of the local church?
In a digital age, yes. The saint can get teachings without being part of
the local church. That is not the local church.

In the local church, we practice esteeming them very highly in love
for their work's sake. Our perspectives, attitudes, slants and practice
of the word are examined by the elders who are accountable for us.

Beyond information acquisition, there is training to practice the word
with others who are also students of the word. It is anticipated that all
in the local assembly we'll be at peace among ourselves as we respond
to the training of our elders.

Where we receive warnings

*14. Now we exhort you, brethren, warn them that are unruly, comfort the
feebleminded, support the weak, be patient toward all men.*
1 Thessalonians 5:14

These brethren, who are to warn the unruly are those charged with oversight over the saints. These are the elders.

There is a place for the elders to warn those who are unruly. These unruly are the men and women who walk contrary to sound doctrine. Thus, the elder does not only teach the word but exercises oversight by watching the saints' conduct in the word.

The independent soul that plans to exist solely by listening to messages and assumes that such a practice is a substitute for the local church, does not understand the God-given role of elders and the local assembly. Real growth happens in the local church.

> 20. *Them that sin rebuke before all, that others also may fear.*
> *1 Timothy 5:20*

Scriptures like "rebuke before all" imply there is a place for all to gather. This "rebuke before all" is so that all may fear. In the absence of such rebuke, the others will receive certain unscriptural actions as acceptable.

Where the saints receive instruction

> 1. *And in those days, when the number of the disciples was multiplied, there arose a murmuring of the Grecians against the Hebrews, because their widows were neglected in the daily ministration. 2. Then the twelve called the multitude of the disciples unto them, and said, It is not reason that we should leave the word of God, and serve tables. 3. Wherefore, brethren, look ye out among you seven men of honest report, full of the Holy Ghost and wisdom, whom we may appoint over this business. 4. But we will give ourselves continually to prayer, and to the ministry of the word. 5. And the saying pleased the whole multitude: and they chose Stephen, a man full of faith and of the Holy Ghost, and Philip, and Prochorus, and Nicanor, and Timon, and Parmenas, and Nicolas a proselyte of*
> *Antioch:*
> *Acts 6:1-5*

The expression "the twelve called the multitude of the disciples unto them," implies that those that are being discipled met for fellowship. More importantly, it means that these disciples recognized the leadership of the twelve. The twelve were the teachers of doctrine (see Acts 2:42).

It was these elders that had taught the disciples that had also instructed the saints, "look out among you for seven men full of the holy spirit".

In addition to teaching them doctrine, the twelve gave instructions to the multitude and the multitude took instructions from the elders. Notice that the apostles' instruction describes the natural aspect of church life. Their instruction implies that in the local church, the people that handle the administration of the natural aspects of church life must be disciples who are firstly given to the word and fluency in the spirit.

"Look out among you" implies there is a coming of saints who are trained in the word together so you can observe excellent service in others who also observe the same in you. This is beyond gaining knowledge. It is the local church.

Where the saint gets taught

16. Wherefore I beseech you, be ye followers of me. 17. For this cause have I sent unto you Timotheus, who is my beloved son, and faithful in the Lord, who shall bring you into remembrance of my ways which be in Christ, as I teach every where in every church.
1 Corinthians 4:16-17

Observe that the custom of Paul was to teach everywhere in every church. This means that Paul's instruction for the saints to be taught the word, requires that strong local churches where these teachings are given. It was to the local church that he sent Timothy, who was to "bring you into remembrance of my ways which be in Christ, as I teach." Timothy's ministry to the Corinthians will be given and received in the local church.

Where "My servants" are raised

41. Then they that gladly received his word were baptized: and the same day there were added unto them about three thousand souls.

Acts 2: 41

As a result of Peter's preaching, 3000 souls got born again. These men were then added to the local church. The fact that their number was known shows you human administration was involved. These are the men who counted the number. That is the territory of the local church.

18. And on my servants and on my handmaidens I will pour out in those days of my Spirit; and they shall prophesy:

Acts 2:18

Peter had explained God's promise through Joel's prophecy. It is God's plan to produce more "My servants" and "My handmaidens".

39. For the promise is unto you, and to your children, and to all that are afar off, even as many as the Lord our God shall call.

Acts 2:39

God's promise is that in the new birth, a man receives the forgiveness of sins in the gift of the Holy Ghost. The man that receives the Holy Ghost is made God's minister.

Those who heard Peter just heard his explanation of Joel's prophecy, by which they just heard was that through salvation they became sons who were "My servants" and "My handmaidens". Therefore, Peter's success would be measured by those 3000 becoming "My servants" and "My handmaidens".

42. And they continued stedfastly in the apostles' doctrine and fellowship, and in breaking of bread, and in prayers.

Acts 2:42

The 3000 continued in apostles' doctrine. This is how the 3000 were to become "My servants".

In Antioch

20. And some of them were men of Cyprus and Cyrene, which, when they were come to Antioch, spake unto the Grecians, preaching the Lord Jesus. 21. And the hand of the Lord was with them: and a great number believed, and turned unto the Lord.
Acts 11:20-21

The disciples preach the Lord Jesus (His resurrection) to Antioch. The great number that believed the gospel received salvation. These were now saints.

22. Then tidings of these things came unto the ears of the church which was in Jerusalem: and they sent forth Barnabas, that he should go as far as Antioch. 23. Who, when he came, and had seen the grace of God, was glad, and exhorted them all, that with purpose of heart they would cleave unto the Lord.
Acts 11:22-23

The apostles in the church at Jerusalem knew that the saints at Antioch needed to be encouraged. They sent a man, Barnabas, for this purpose. When Barnabas came, the expression "had seen the grace of God" means that he saw that they had received eternal life.

The exhortation about the purposing in their heart to cleave unto the Lord means that now that they were saved, discipleship was needed.

25. Then departed Barnabas to Tarsus, for to seek Saul: 26. And when he had found him, he brought him unto Antioch. And it came to pass, that a whole year they assembled themselves with the church, and taught much people. And the disciples were called Christians first in Antioch.
Acts 11:25-26

It was Barnabas and Saul that assembled themselves with the church.

Which church was this? This was the church at Antioch. Barnabas and Paul did not tell the universal church to gather to receive teaching. Thus, teaching is given at the local church level. It was in this assembling themselves with others that they taught the people.

Observe that "assembled themselves with the church" and "taught much people" are one and the same thing. The assembly was in order that the saints might be trained to becoming disciples by teaching them the word. So, to assemble the church is to teach them.

The local church is where the saints are taught together. It is in the local church that the saint is separated from the ignorance of the scriptures. The saints are to be taught together with other saints.

It was these disciples that were called Christians. The saints did not call themselves Christians per se. They were disciples, trained in the doctrine of Christ. People saw discipleship and referred to it as "Christians."

It was the saints who were well-taught by elders in the local assembly that the people referred to as Christians.

They saw disciples. They called them Christians.

The local church exists to make disciples of saints. Man's natural wisdom has worked out how to build amusement centres. Men already know how entertainment works. They do not need the church to create more amusement centres.

19. Go ye therefore, and teach all nations, baptizing them in the name of the Father, and of the Son, and of the Holy Ghost:
Matthew 28:19

The KJV's rendering of Matthew's recapturing of Jesus' lasts words were "Go ye therefore and teach all nations". The word translated "teach" in "teach all nations" means to produce students. Thus, you can summarise the Lord's assignment in two words "make disciples." Those are our marching orders. We are to make disciples.

In Antioch, we see that this is done by teaching men and women in the local assembly. The teaching and instructions by elders is a way of fulfilling the Lord's plan of populating the earth with His disciples.

45. Then opened he their understanding, that they might understand the scriptures,
Luke 24:45

In Luke 24, Jesus taught the scriptures and by it He opened the understanding of those men who gave Him attention. We follow His example in the local church. All the labour of the local church is for the understanding of men to be opened by the word rightly taught.

Is being taught from afar not enough? The digital age shows that it is very possible to be taught the word from afar. We must not confuse this for discipleship. Discipleship involves a heavy exposure to men and women who teach us, watch over our practice of the word and who influence us by their practice of the word.

The local church fills the big void in the world – the making of disciples of Christ.

God's plan is for us to hear the glorious truths of the redemption that we have in Christ, and in doing so we follow this rigorously with the life of service as our example in Christ Jesus.

An understanding of the fact that the church is the ground and pillar of truth influences the way the saint thinks of the church and prepares for its meetings.

In the local church, scriptures come alive, the instruction of the scriptures is explained, scriptural instructions and warning are given and the Epistles are practised together by all. Therefore, it is in the local church that we can tell the development of the saint.

2. Preach the word; be instant in season, out of season; reprove, rebuke, exhort with all longsuffering and doctrine. 3. For the time will come when they will not endure sound doctrine; but after their own lusts shall they heap to themselves

teachers, having itching ears; 4. And they shall turn away their ears from the
truth, and shall be turned unto fables.
2 Timothy 4:2-4

Paul's command to Timothy was "Preach the word" and to "reprove, rebuke and exhort". He let Timothy know that these are to be carried out "with all longsuffering."

Longsuffering is involved in doctrine.

The local church is the theater for training men to endure sound doctrine. Good doctrine is not always exciting – it is often not. However, Good doctrine is good and men need to be trained to abide by sound doctrine. The world thrives on itchy ears, but the saint is not the world.

Influence of godly example

10. But thou hast fully known my doctrine, manner of life, purpose, faith, longsuffering, charity, patience, 11. Persecutions, afflictions, which came unto me at Antioch, at Iconium, at Lystra; what persecutions I endured: but out of them all the Lord delivered me. 12. Yea, and all that will live godly in Christ Jesus shall suffer persecution.
2 Timothy 3:10-12

Paul reminds Timothy that Timothy had been discipled tremendously by what he had heard Paul teach and what he had seen him act out in the conduct of that doctrine.

9. Those things, which ye have both learned, and received, and heard, and seen in me, do: and the God of peace shall be with you.
Philippians 4:9

The Philippians are disciples of Paul. He wrote these to them as an assembly.

They had heard Paul's teaching. They had also seen the example of that doctrine in him. Paul instructs the saints to do what they had heard in his teaching and seen in his example. The local assembly distinguishes itself as the place where saints are exposed to godly influences and examples.

The local assembly excels in three things - Hear. See. Do.

1. The elders which are among you I exhort, who am also an elder, and a witness of the sufferings of Christ, and also a partaker of the glory that shall be revealed: 2. Feed the flock of God which is among you, taking the oversight thereof, not by constraint, but willingly; not for filthy lucre, but of a ready mind; 3. Neither as being lords over God's heritage, but being ensamples to the flock.
1 Peter 5:1-3

The Elders are among the saints. They are overseers whose oversight means that they are ensamples to the flock. Elders also supply both teaching and example to the saints. Disciples receive the teaching of the elders and follow the example seen in the godly conduct of the elders.

Some saints are not disciples because they only listen to teaching but do not expose themselves to godly examples of elders. There are bad elders that only teach, while ignoring or downplaying the pivotal responsibility of the elders to show a godly example to the saints.

Any saint who has heard teachings, and who has a good memory can regurgitate teaching. As scary as it seems, even an unbeliever can regurgitate facts listened to.

What of saints who desire to teach? This is good and welcome. Such a desire is needed so that we can reach the lost with the gospel. However, such saints need to be trained to exemplify sound doctrine to other saints.

Can a saint want to teach but be grossly lacking in being an example? Yes. That's where we all start. We all start there but should let the word strip us of poor conduct.

Is such a saint ready to be an elder? No. Over and above knowing the word, the elder is a chief example setter to the saints in the local church.

What of an elder who wants to teach but ignores being an example of the doctrine? Such an elder is disobeying Peter's command to the elders. The terms "Elder" and "poor conduct" should not go together. The Pharisees were this way. You were a bit safe with what the Pharisees said, but you would turn out badly following what they do.

Is teaching not enough? No. It is not. If all that the saints needed was teaching, there would be no need for elders who are commanded to be examples to the flock. Think about it. Elders are critical for our growth because they should be mature enough to adorn the doctrine in their conduct and train others to do the same.

What happens when there is teaching but no godly example? Peter says the elder would lord it over the saints.

People who are taught but who are robbed of seeing the example of it in those who have taught them the word have also been robbed of the godly influence that is actively required in discipleship.

3. Giving no offence in any thing, that the ministry be not blamed:
2 Corinthians 6:3

The gospel is the power of God to save (see Romans 1:16) and also the power of God for transforming the minds of the saints (see Romans 12:2). If the elder is not an example of the conduct of sacrifice found in Christ, the ministry will be blamed and the minister's conduct might distract the people from focusing on the gospel.

5. For our gospel came not unto you in word only, but also in power, and in the
Holy Ghost, and in much assurance; as ye know what manner of men we were
among you for your sake.
1 Thessalonians 1:5

Paul, who brought the gospel to the Thessalonians said, "ye know what manner of men we were among you for your sake". So there is a manner associated with the elders. It is for the benefit of the saints.

12. Let no man despise thy youth; but be thou an example of the believers, in word, in conversation, in charity, in spirit, in faith, in purity.
1 Timothy 4:12

Timothy was well-reported of by the brethren that were at Lystra and Iconium (see Acts 16:1-2).

"Thy youth" shows that Timothy is young

"Despise thy youth" implies do not act your age.

"Let no man despise thy youth" implies that Timothy was unusual on account of his youthfulness. The elders tended to be older men.

"Let no man despise thy youth" is not up to the saints. It is up to the pastor who turns things around by not acting his or her age but instead acts revelation knowledge.

Although some people might look up to Timothy and other people might look down on him, Paul lets Timothy know that the elder can turn it around. Timothy could do something about it by giving himself to sound doctrine and showing his maturity in his conduct. He is to be an example. He would use sound doctrine and its conduct to open the hearts of people to him.

Paul says, "let no man despise thy youth." He does not say that it is a sin to be younger than your congregation.

The man who exercises oversight in the local assembly by training them in the gospel is to be an example of God's love to the saints. The elder who has presented a perfect Saviour to the saints is now told to present Him in the conduct of a sound doctrine.

Paul does not tell Timothy to let no man despise your youth by concealing or inflating your age. Let no man despise thy youth does not mean to refer to saints who are older than you as "sons" and "daughters." Paul points out to Timothy the self-evident fact that Timothy has older men and older women in the assembly that Timothy pastors. There is a way to handle people in the local assembly (see 1 Timothy 5:1-2).

Paul lets the elder know that the elder who is not an example of sound doctrine sets himself or herself up for unnecessary troubles in the local assembly.

The fact is that Timothy was youthful but proven.

The elder should act the word and not age, culture, gender, or his title. The elder presents revelation knowledge and acts it out for the saints to see. This motivates and influences the saints. The elders' example is how the elder rebukes worldly slants in the saints.

The truth is in God's saints. The saints are instructed in this with other saints in the local assembly where the elders show us by their example. Without this godly example, we might not walk in the instructions that we already know in the scriptures.

Although we believers are possessors of eternal life, we need examples to follow. The elders must be these examples. The fact is that people become persuaded not only by what they hear taught, they continually develop persuasion by the examples that they are continually exposed to.

Here's what Paul said:

17. Did I make a gain of you by any of them whom I sent unto you? 18. I desired Titus, and with him I sent a brother. Did Titus make a gain of you? walked we not in the same spirit? walked we not in the same steps?
2 Corinthians 12:17-18

Observe that the elders are men of sound conduct. The leader does not take advantage of anyone under their care. Paul's conduct influenced Titus and Paul expected Titus' conduct to influence the Corinthians. No wonder Paul boasted that they walked in the same steps.

The local church is how God meets the great need of producing disciples of Christ. It is the only endeavor that solely exists to train the saints as disciples of Christ.

Everyone is a product of influence. We are always being influenced. Therefore, in the local assembly there are men whose examples we follow in order that we might receive the service of Christ.

Where elders emerge

2. And the things that thou hast heard of me among many witnesses, the same commit thou to faithful men, who shall be able to teach others also.
2 Timothy 2:2

Paul did not give this instruction to everyone. He committed this charge to Timothy, who was to watch out for faithful men in the local church. Timothy was to see to it that he commits the gospel to faithful men. This committing of the gospel is done by the elders in the local church. It is the faithful men that should be trained to teach others in the local church.

5. For this cause left I thee in Crete, that thou shouldest set in order the things that are wanting, and ordain elders in every city, as I had appointed thee: 6. If any be blameless, the husband of one wife, having faithful children not accused of riot or unruly. 7. For a bishop must be blameless, as the steward of God; not selfwilled, not soon angry, not given to wine, no striker, not given to filthy lucre; 8. But a lover of hospitality, a lover of good men, sober, just, holy, temperate; 9. Holding fast the faithful word as he hath been taught, that he may be able by sound doctrine both to exhort and to convince the gainsayers.
Titus 1:5-9

Titus was to be in the local churches and from amongst the saints, ordain men to eldership.

All the qualifications required of the elders require close observation in face-to-face fellowship.

Where service is proven

10. And let these also first be proved; then let them use the office of a deacon,
being found blameless.
1 Timothy 3:10

The local church is where we first prove our service. This is the purpose of the ordination of deacons.

3. Wherefore, brethren, look ye out among you seven men of honest report, full
of the Holy Ghost and wisdom, whom we may appoint over this business. 4. But
we will give ourselves continually to prayer, and to the ministry of the word. 5.
And the saying pleased the whole multitude: and they chose Stephen, a man full
of faith and of the Holy Ghost, and Philip, and Prochorus, and Nicanor, and
Timon, and Parmenas, and Nicolas a proselyte of Antioch: 6. Whom they set
before the apostles: and when they had prayed, they laid their hands on them.
Acts 6:3-6

This execution of this instruction is only possible where people relate with one another and see each other frequently.

Do you observe that the selection of the deacons was not by prayer? All the qualifications that the elders had said were required in these men could be validated by other saints in the local church. The apostles' instruction required that the saints had extended fellowship with one another. This is because an honest reputation is built over time where others can see you up, close and personal. This also implies that though God does not relate with us based on our conduct, we watch out for those in whom we see service and sound conduct when we meet.

So, the people were selected based on observation in the local assembly. The prayer was only to separate those who had distinguished themselves in service. The seven men in Acts 6 did not go on a campaign, asking to be made leaders.

The training not to despise other saints

2. For if there come unto your assembly a man with a gold ring, in goodly apparel, and there come in also a poor man in vile raiment;
3. And ye have respect to him that weareth the gay clothing, and say unto him, Sit thou here in a good place; and say to the poor, Stand thou there, or sit here under my footstool: 4. Are ye not then partial in yourselves, and are become judges of evil thoughts? 5. Hearken, my beloved brethren, Hath not God chosen the poor of this world rich in faith, and heirs of the kingdom which he hath promised to them that love him?
James 2:2-5

When James says, "if there come unto your assembly", he is speaking of the saints coming together in the local church with other saints. He is training them in the manners of the saints in the local assembly. We know it cannot be the universal church because the universal church is spiritual, while the gold ring is earthly materiality. He also speaks of the poor man in vile raiment. As we already know, all saints are made rich in the new man.

As the elder, what James was teaching here was for the saints not to despise other saints on account of their being poor saints (see James 2:6). We learn to get along with each other as saints.

20. When ye come together therefore into one place, this is not to eat the Lord's supper. 21. For in eating every one taketh before other his own supper: and one is hungry, and another is drunken. 22. What? have ye not houses to eat and to drink in? or despise ye the church of God, and shame them that have not? What shall I say to you? shall I praise you in this? I praise you not.
1 Corinthians 11:20-22

Paul is discussing what happens "When ye come together therefore into one place." This one place refers to where the local church. He distinguishes between what is permissible in personal houses and what is permissible in the local church. It is in the local church that the saints learn not to despise those that have not. It is where the saint learns not to shame them that have not. As saints, it is in the local church, that we relate emphasizing those things given us in Christ.

It is in the local church that men are separated to ministry

> *1. Now there were in the church that was at Antioch certain prophets and teachers; as Barnabas, and Simeon that was called Niger, and Lucius of Cyrene, and Manaen, which had been brought up with Herod the tetrarch, and Saul. 2. As they ministered to the Lord, and fasted, the Holy Ghost said, Separate me Barnabas and Saul for the work whereunto I have called them. 3. And when they had fasted and prayed, and laid their hands on them, they sent them away. 4. So they, being sent forth by the Holy Ghost, departed unto Seleucia; and from thence they sailed to Cyprus.*
> *Acts 13:1-4*

This is the separation of Barnabas and Paul to apostolic ministry. While God had called Barnabas and Paul to a work, it was men that separated them to it in the local church. This did not happen in the desert but in the church that was at Antioch. We can see therefore that the local church was where Barnabas and Paul were separated unto a work to discharge in the Lord.

This giving of self to ministry is what it means to give with simplicity (see Romans 12:8). Barnabas and Paul are giving service to the saints from the measure of faith (see Romans 12:3).

We are trained to become givers in the local church. This is not just giving of our material resources but the giving of ourselves in service and ministry.

Observe that when the elders had separated Barnabas and Paul by praying for them and sending them away, the Holy Ghost is said to have sent them forth! Evidently, God acts by the elders that He has set in the local churches. In fact, it is impossible to be in the will of God and stay away from the local church.

How we adorn the gospel in everyday life

> *9. Exhort servants to be obedient unto their own masters, and to please them*

well in all things; not answering again; 10. Not purloining, but shewing all good
fidelity; that they may adorn the doctrine of God our Saviour in all things.
Titus 2:9-10

Paul instructs Titus to exhort the saints about their relationships outside the local church!

In this scenario, the elders are to teach the saints to adorn the doctrine
of God by their conduct seen in their relation to their managers in
the commercial setting. We are to adorn the doctrine of God in all
the things done in the office. Though the commercial sphere is not
spiritual and is governed by the wisdom of man, as saints, our conduct
in it is spiritual. Thus, the elder trains the saints that real spirituality
is not seen only in our meetings in the local church. Whatever we do,
saints are always subject to the law of Christ (see 1 Corinthians 9:21).

Why does Paul give these commands?

11. God's marvelous grace has manifested in person, bringing salvation for
everyone
Titus 2:11 (TPT)

The foundation for Paul's instructions regarding the saint's conduct is
because the grace of God has appeared. This is by eternal life, which
is in us and which we have received by believing the gospel. This grace
in us (eternal life) instructs us to walk in the spirit, making us able to
reign over worldly lusts. Submission to the training received by the
elders in the local church means that we adorn the doctrine of God
in our secular affairs.

Therefore, our conduct is a consequence of eternal life in us. There
is sound conduct in God's life within. As the saints get instructed in
the gospel, the understanding of the word means that our thinking no
longer resists the expression of that conduct. If a man is truly given
to sound doctrine, the apostles assure us that it will be seen in his conduct in his relationships even outside the local church.

Nevertheless, many think that the saint finds spirituality only by spending all their time in those "spiritual" activities conducted within the local church.

Paul commanded Timothy along similar lines:

1. Let as many servants as are under the yoke count their own masters worthy of all honour, that the name of God and his doctrine be not blasphemed.

1 Timothy 6:1

"Servants as are under the yoke," refers to the natural sphere of life. This is the commercial sphere. In the local church, the elder teaches the saints, who are servants, to "count their own masters worthy of all honour." There is saintly conduct in the commercial sphere.

The elder is to be interested in the conduct of the saints in the commercial sphere. There is a tendency in some quarters, to separate between the secular and the spiritual aspects of the saint's life in such a way that the saint assumes that conduct in the secular sphere is outside the reach of sound instructions in the word. Paul tackles this. The pastor is to be concerned about the way that the saints handle the natural sphere of life. If this is not taught by the elders in the local church, the name of God and his doctrine would be blasphemed!

The pastor is to know and keep abreast of the conduct of the saints in the work sphere. Therefore, the pastor will not assemble the saints in the local church in such a way that in order to meet the demands of assembly, the saints are unable to fulfil their obligations towards their masters. In effect, the saints blaspheme the name of God and sound doctrine by not having a good testimony before men.

So, it is in the local church that the elder teaches the saints that the conduct of spirituality is seen in the manner of the saint in the commercial space.

Paul's instructions to Timothy

12. Let no man despise thy youth; but be thou an example of the believers, in word, in conversation, in charity, in spirit, in faith, in purity.
1 Timothy 4:12

As a pastor in a local assembly setting, Timothy is to be an example unto the believers. The saints are the recipients of his example.

1 Don't be harsh or verbally abusive to an older man; it is better to appeal to him as a father. And as you minister to the younger men it is best to encourage them as your dear brothers. 2 Honor the older women as mothers, and the younger women, treat as your dear sisters with utmost purity.
1 Timothy 5:1-2 (TPT)

Timothy's example is seen in the way that he handles relationships with other saints. There is a way he is to engage the older saints as well as the younger.

Paul's instructions in 1 Timothy 5 shows that as pastors, we must not maintain a detachment from the natural aspects of people's lives.

8. But if any provide not for his own, and specially for those of his own house, he hath denied the faith, and is worse than an infidel.
1 Timothy 5:8

Paul teaches Timothy that the Christian should take care of his own house.

What is Paul referring to?

3. Honour widows that are widows indeed.
1 Timothy 5:3

Timothy is to see to it that "widows indeed" are honoured. How are they honoured?

16. If any man or woman that believeth have widows, let them relieve them, and let not the church be charged; that it may relieve them that are widows indeed.

1 Timothy 5:16

The local church honours those who are "widows indeed" by caring for them. This honour refers to reverence and material support. What does the "any man or woman that believeth" have? They have widows.

8. But if any provide not for his own, and specially for those of his own house, he hath denied the faith, and is worse than an infidel.

1 Timothy 5:8

Careful attention to detail shows that "his own" in "provide not for his own" refers to the widow(s) that the "man or woman that believeth" is responsible towards. So, Paul commands Timothy to charge the younger saints to take care of their older family members. Saints that fail to take care of their aged parents are worse than infidels who have denied the faith (sound doctrine).

Can a pastor be this involved in the lives of the saints in the local assembly? Yes. When a pastor is not as involved as instructed in the pastoral epistles but assumes that only certain "spiritual" things are in scope, the pastor is not heeding Paul's charge.

Now, when Paul speaks of saints who are worse than unbelievers, he is not referring to their loss of eternal life. "Worse than an infidel" has to do with the handling of natural relationships (in context, care of widows). The saint is "worse than an unbeliever" because infidels understand the necessity of caring for family members. Therefore, it is grossly poor conduct if the saint refuses to care for elderly ones. This "worse than infidels" refers to saints who do not regulate their natural relationships by the word.

Timothy's oversight means that he watches out for the way the saints practised the conduct of sound doctrine in their natural relationships. The elders are not to be detached from the way that the saints practice the doctrine they have been taught.

Paul went into great detail in his instructions on the procedure concerning the care for widows:

3. Honour widows that are widows indeed. 4. But if any widow have children or nephews, let them learn first to shew piety at home, and to requite their parents: for that is good and acceptable before God. 5. Now she that is a widow indeed, and desolate, trusteth in God, and continueth in supplications and prayers night and day.6. But she that liveth in pleasure is dead while she liveth. 7. And these things give in charge, that they may be blameless. 8. But if any provide not for his own, and specially for those of his own house, he hath denied the faith, and is worse than an infidel. 9. Let not a widow be taken into the number under threescore years old, having been the wife of one man, 10. Well reported of for good works; if she have brought up children, if she have lodged strangers, if she have washed the saints' feet, if she have relieved the afflicted, if she have diligently followed every good work. 11. But the younger widows refuse: for when they have begun to wax wanton against Christ, they will marry; 12. Having damnation, because they have cast off their first faith. 13. And withal they learn to be idle, wandering about from house to house; and not only idle, but tattlers also and busybodies, speaking things which they ought not. 14. I will therefore that the younger women marry, bear children, guide the house, give none occasion to the adversary to speak reproachfully. 15. For some are already turned aside after Satan. 16. If any man or woman that believeth have widows, let them relieve them, and let not the church be charged; that it may relieve them that are widows indeed.
1 Timothy 5:3-16

Paul is instructing Timothy on those things that the elder of the local church should consider before taking up full responsibility for the care of a widow! He is teaching on how to honour widows that are widows indeed. The points he makes require that the pastor is to know the conduct of the flock outside the local church very well. He says, "Let not a widow be taken into the number under threescore years old". He is even to know their age.

"Taken into the number" means the local church assumes full responsibility. There is a difference between the church helping occasionally and the church assuming full responsibility of the care of the widows.

The detailed instruction to Timothy do not govern giving once in a while to support these widows.

It is open to debate whether Paul has 60 years in mind literally or whether that is a parabolic reference to the fact that that they are old enough to no longer be part of an active workforce. It appears he sets this to show that these women are dependent on others for financial upkeep as they can no longer work.

This is a staggering degree of detail that Paul wants Timothy to get into, where the natural sphere of the saints is concerned. Timothy is to get involved in the lives of these widows and their believing relatives in the local church. If Paul gets into such detail, and Timothy is like-minded, it means that Timothy would be very detailed about the lives of the flock. Paul trained Timothy to enter a great degree of detail about the family members of these widows who are saints. He was expected to know if the saints were taking care of their widows.

16. If any man or woman that believeth have widows, let them relieve them, and let not the church be charged; that it may relieve them that are widows indeed.
1 Timothy 5:16

In the local church, the elder is to know the relationships between the saints, understand the dynamics of their relationships and determine whether a believer who has widows is taking full responsibility for their care. These are patterns that are observable when saints gather face to face and elders create an atmosphere where people watch out for one another. The saints are not just listening to teaching in their houses, they are available to gather with other saints, to be taught with other saints by elders who get involved in their practice of doctrine in their everyday lives.

7. Be sure to give clear instruction concerning these matters so that none of them will live with shame.
1 Timothy 5:7 (TPT)

The pastor is to charge or command the saints who have widows to take full support in their care of them in the natural sphere of life.

Paul says that Timothy is to charge or give clear instruction about this. Those saints who have widows are to heed Timothy's charge. The saint will not say, "it is up to me what I do, whether I care for my widows or not." The well-taught saint will not say that. The local assembly is to continuously monitor these things.

8. But if any provide not for his own, and specially for those of his own house, he hath denied the faith, and is worse than an infidel.
1 Timothy 5:8

The saint that does not heed this charge to fully support his or her widows is worse than an infidel and has denied the faith. This means that such a saint is opposing the sound doctrine received in the local church by his or her negligence of those under his or her care.

16. If any man or woman that believeth have widows, let them relieve them, and let not the church be charged; that it may relieve them that are widows indeed.
1 Timothy 5:16

"Let not the church be charged" means that Paul's instructions are directed at the elders in the local church. Although these instructions have to do with the private life of the saints, because these things have a bearing on the practice of sound doctrine, the pastor is involved. It is the pastor that enforces these instructions in the local assembly.

If the saints who have believing widows care for their widows, their excellent conduct frees up the local assembly to care for those that are widows indeed. The saint acts this way because he or she understands that the local church should not relieve a saint of personal responsibility. The church frees up its resources to care for those who are widows indeed.

Should it not be up to the "man or woman that believeth" who have believing widows whether they care for their widows or not? Apparently not. This, that we would classify as a personal domain, is a sphere where the pastor is instructed to command the "man or woman that believeth" on what to do in this situation. Such is the gravity of the role of the elder. It requires an elder who is an example of the doctrine.

Paul teaches concerning the saints who have widows, "let them learn first to shew piety at home" (see 1 Tim. 5:4). This learning takes place in the local church. It is an impact of the gospel and the elder watches out for it. This learning concerns conduct at home.

It is far easier for the elder to turn a blind eye, leave the saints who do not care for their household alone and have the church assume the care of such. The elder that does this is enabling such saints to be worse than infidels. Soon, such an elder leads an assembly of saints who are worse than infidels. It becomes difficult to establish whether it is the elders who cannot rebuke and correct by the word or it is the saints who do not receive correction by the word.

We observe that In 1st Timothy 5, the elder teaches the personal responsibility of the saints in caring for their widows, charges the local church to train the saints to care for their relatives, rebukes those saints who choose not to care for their relatives, and informs on the characteristics of those the church is to support. He even explains what the care for the younger widows looks like. If they are still young, it is anticipated that those that married before would likely marry again. The church supports in a way that would not aid idleness but free up to serve others.

What does Paul mean by "widows indeed"?

5. Now she that is a widow indeed, and desolate, trusteth in God, and continueth in supplications and prayers night and day.
1 Timothy 5:5

The "widow indeed" is the widow who is in need and is desolate. Here, "desolate" means she is without relatives who care for her. Paul commands Timothy to teach that all who are not widows indeed are to be cared for by their believing relatives who are saints in the local church. The believing relatives that ignore this or neglect to take responsibility are worse than an infidel (see 1 Timothy 5:8,16).

Some scholars argue that these "widow indeed" are those whose husband was killed due to the persecution of believers.

Paul gives further details about widows indeed:

10. Well reported of for good works; if she have brought up children, if she have lodged strangers, if she have washed the saints' feet, if she have relieved the afflicted, if she have diligently followed every good work.
1 Timothy 5:10

The "widows indeed" are not just those without believing relatives to support them, they meet other requirements laid down by Paul. "If she have diligently followed every good work" captures the sentiment Paul expressed using many other words. It means that this widow is a proven disciple and not an opportunist.

11. As for younger widows, do not put them on such a list. For when their sensual desires overcome their dedication to Christ, they want to marry;
1 Timothy 5:11 (NIV)

What of younger widows who want to be seen as "widows indeed"?

Paul instructs Timothy to refuse them that care that should be reserved for those who are widows in deed!

However, observe that Paul teaches or explains while giving these commands.

14 For this reason, teach the younger women to remarry and bear children and care for their household. This will keep them from giving our adversary a reason to gloat.
1 Timothy 5:14 (TPT)

He teaches that the younger women remarry rather than operating as idle women who "wander about from house to house; and not only idle but tattlers also and busybodies, speaking things which they ought not" (verse 13).

The saint is to anticipate that the elders would be interested in their practice of the word, even outside the local church meetings.

The actions that characterize the local church

The local church is "the house of God, the pillar and ground of the truth" (1 Timothy 3:15), where "this epistle is read among you" (Colossians 4:16-17) and taught (1 Corinthians 4:17), and the saints gather to pray (Acts 1:14;2:1,42), as they feed on sound doctrine (Acts 20:28). It is where we "provoke unto love and to good works" (Hebrews 10:24-25), "ye come together, every one of you hath a psalm, hath a doctrine, hath a tongue, hath a revelation" (1 Corinthians 14:26) and we recognise men fit for ministry (Acts 6:3-6), and these mature men are ordained to the ministry (Acts 14:23;6:6). It is where disagreement among the saints are settled (1 Corinthians 6:4), the saints learn not to despise the church of God (1 Corinthians 11:20-22) and we distribute to meet the material needs of the saints (Acts 4:34-37;11:29-30). It is where the saints receive correction and are exposed to the example of elders who exercise oversight (1 Peter 5:2-3). It is not a multi-purpose event centre.

Discernment & Honour

36. And Joses, who by the apostles was surnamed Barnabas, (which is, being interpreted, The son of consolation,) a Levite, and of the country of Cyprus, 37. Having land, sold it, and brought the money, and laid it at the apostles' feet.
Acts 4:36-37

B arnabas was a disciple who followed the doctrine of the apostles. He was known to them by name.

Barnabas introduced Paul

26. And when Saul was come to Jerusalem, he assayed to join himself to the disciples: but they were all afraid of him, and believed not that he was a disciple. 27. But Barnabas took him, and brought him to the apostles, and declared unto them how he had seen the Lord in the way, and that he had spoken to him, and how he had preached boldly at Damascus in the name of Jesus.
Acts 9:26-27

It was Barnabas who took Paul under his wings and introduced him to the apostles.

22. News of what was happening in Antioch reached the church of Jerusalem, so the apostles sent Barnabas to Antioch as their emissary
Acts 11:22 (TPT)

The Jerusalem church sent Barnabas to Antioch.

Barnabas and Paul assembled the saints

25. Then departed Barnabas to Tarsus, for to seek Saul: 26. And when he had found him, he brought him unto Antioch. And it came to pass, that a whole year they assembled themselves with the church, and taught much people. And the disciples were called Christians first in Antioch.
Acts 11:25-26

Barnabas it was who went after Paul and invited him to be an elder in Antioch church. Thus, In Antioch, Barnabas was the more senior elder. The recognized teacher sent from the Jerusalem church. Together, both men assembled the saints in the local church and taught the people for 1 year.

1. Fourteen years later I returned to Jerusalem, this time with Barnabas and Titus, my coworkers. 2 God had given me a clear revelation to go and confer with the other apostles concerning the message of grace I was preaching to the non-Jewish people. I spoke privately with those who were viewed as senior leaders of the church. I wanted to make certain that my labor and ministry for the Messiah had not been based on a false understanding of the gospel. 3 They even accepted Titus without demanding that he follow strict Jewish customs before they would receive him as a brother since he was a Syrian and not a Jew.
Galatians 2:1-3 (TPT)

When Barnabas and Paul went to Jerusalem, Peter, James and John heard the gospel that Paul preached. Peter, James and John knew the truth, so no one asked Titus to be circumcised. Thus, the teaching of Barnabas and Paul to there the disciples at Antioch was validated.

26. And when he had found him, he brought him unto Antioch. And it came to pass, that a whole year they assembled themselves with the church, and taught much people. And the disciples were called Christians first in Antioch.
Acts 11:26

The people were so well taught and discipled, that a new name was coined for them. It was a church of disciples. Men that were given to sound doctrine.

Peter was to be blamed

11 But when Cephas came to Antioch, I opposed him to his face, because he had clearly done wrong. 12 Until certain people came from James, he had been eating with the Gentiles. But when they arrived, he stopped doing this and separated himself because he was afraid of those who were pro-circumcision.
Galatians 2:11-12 (NET)

When Peter came to Antioch, he acted on the truth of scriptures until his fear of certain that had come from James caused him to withdraw and separate himself. For this, Paul affirmed that Peter "had clearly done wrong".

13. And the rest of the Jews also joined with him in this hypocrisy, so that even Barnabas was led astray with them by their hypocrisy.
Galatians 2:13 (NET)

Peter's actions influenced the other Jews. He should have been the shepherd protecting them from these men from James, but instead acted in fear. Peter's actions also influenced Barnabas, who was the pastor at Antioch! Paul's "even Barnabas was led astray with them by their hypocrisy" means that he was more shocked that Peter could influence Barnabas this way. This helps us understand the issues at stake when Paul said that Peter was worthy of blame.

It is blameworthy when the pastor of a local assembly is hooked by unsound teachings and practices.

Who acted publicly? Paul said, "I opposed him to his face." Paul acted quickly. This is Paul the apostle withstanding Peter the apostle to the face. They are both ministers.

Barnabas was carried away or influenced by what Peter did. The man that had taught Barnabas the grace of God was walking contrary to that grace. Where Paul had concluded that Peter was to be blamed, Barnabas did not see blame in Peter's action. He fell in line. Peter was the teacher of the man that Paul had supported in the Antioch church. Yet, Paul saw the same men that Peter had been afraid of but Paul was not fearful.

Paul rebuked Peter

14. But when I saw that they walked not uprightly according to the truth of the gospel, I said unto Peter before them all, If thou, being a Jew, livest after the manner of Gentiles, and not as do the Jews, why compellest thou the Gentiles to live as do the Jews?
Galatians 2:14

Paul did not let any of the saints in Antioch withstand Peter to the face. That would be dishonourable. There are other saints who might have reached the same conclusions that Paul had reached. However, the saints would be required to protect his mind and heart from Peter's influence. The saint would not be expected to withstand Peter in the assembly because the care of the assembled saints at Antioch is committed to Barnabas and Paul.

These saints were not supposed to withstand Peter to the face as Paul did. They were to learn from how Paul handled the situation. They would learn that although the elders have oversight, the elders are not always right. The saints would learn that just like every other saint, all the elders are subject to the truth of the gospel. However, there is a way to go about correcting the elder who is in error.

One of the God-given roles of elders is that they are best placed to rebuke other elders where the actions of those elders directly affect the local assembly.

Paul said that Peter, Pastor Barnabas and the other Jewish ministers had not walked uprightly according to the truth of the very gospel that Peter and Pastor Barnabas knew. This is the gospel that Peter had agreed with in the Galatians 2:1 Jerusalem meeting. The very gospel that Barnabas had taught in Antioch for a year.

Paul was not carried away.

8. For he that wrought effectually in Peter to the apostleship of the circumcision, the same was mighty in me toward the Gentiles:) 9. And when James, Cephas, and John, who seemed to be pillars, perceived the grace that was given unto me, they gave to me and Barnabas the right hands of fellowship; that we should go unto the heathen, and they unto the circumcision.
Galatians 2:8-9

Peter knew both Barnabas and Paul and perceived the grace that was given unto Paul. How did Paul handle this?

14. But when I saw that they walked not uprightly according to the truth of the gospel, I said unto Peter before them all, If thou, being a Jew, livest after the manner of Gentiles, and not as do the Jews, why compellest thou the Gentiles to live as do the Jews?
Galatians 2:14

The fact that Barnabas was "carried away with their dissimulation", and that Peter was leading the dissimulation did not stop Paul from judging on the matter in the Antioch church.

Paul did not judge by the personalities involved. He subjected all the elders involved to whether they walked uprightly according to the truth of the gospel or not. Paul said, "I said unto Peter before them all"

Again, although Peter's actions had directly affected the saints at Antioch, it was not the saints that "said unto Peter before them all". Paul corrected Peter and Barnabas before all those who had been affected by Peter's actions.

Paul's correction was public because the error had been public and the saints had been exposed to the actions of Peter and Pastor Barnabas.

Paul, the outsider and associate, who Barnabas had invited to partner in the ministry that the Jerusalem church tasked him with, was now correcting Peter who had sent Barnabas to Antioch – this is not politically correct. However, it is scriptural. The local church is not run by political correctness.

Faithfulness is expected of stewards. The gospel is to be committed to faithful men (see 2 Timothy 2:2).

Paul's teaching to the Galatians shows that elders are best placed to rebuke and correct other elders. While the elders are correcting one another, the saints learn from the elders. The correction was public because the error had been public.

Peter's importance

Why had Paul spoken to Peter and not to anyone else? Paul would have spoken to Peter because he knew Peter's importance. He withstood Peter's action because Peter's action galvanized the other elders, including Barnabas who was the pastor of the church at Antioch. In Peter's repentance, the other elders would trace their own repentance.

Elders are examples

3. Neither as being lords over God's heritage, but being ensamples to the flock.
1 Peter 5:3

The elder is to be an example.

In Peter's response to Paul's rebuke, the saints in Antioch would be persuaded by Peter's example of submission to the word and in his repentance, the saints will learn how to receive corrections.

In the Galatians 2 issue at Antioch, Paul is also taking oversight by showing the saints the example of giving the word first place and prioritizing the word over personalities.

If the saints are well taught, the saints should have known that Barnabas had been wrong to follow Peter's poor example. This is discernment, a quality all disciples should have.

Given that these events had happened previously in Antioch, and that Peter had since repented, why is Paul bringing it up in the letter to the Galatians?

Let him be accursed

> *6. I marvel that ye are so soon removed from him that called you into the grace of Christ unto another gospel: 7. Which is not another; but there be some that trouble you, and would pervert the gospel of Christ. 8. But though we, or an angel from heaven, preach any other gospel unto you than that which we have preached unto you, let him be accursed. 9. As we said before, so say I now again, If any man preach any other gospel unto you than that ye have received, let him be accursed.*
> *Galatians 1:6-9*

Paul includes himself in the "If any man". He is emphatic on the scriptural responsibility of each saint to judge the things that are taught to him or her. Paul does not tell the saints at Galatia to examine his words so as to rebuke him.

The saints at Galatia were being troubled by preachers who were preaching another gospel.

Paul's "If any man preach any other gospel unto you than that ye have received" means that he wanted the Galatians to know that just as they had been responsible for receiving the gospel when Paul had brought it to them originally, they were still responsible for receiving what Paul or any other minister was showing them from scriptures.

Although Paul taught them the scriptures, Paul lets them know that what he says is to be subject to the very gospel he had preached to them at the first.

Which elders did Paul exempt

Paul's "'if any man preach any other gospel unto you than that ye have received" shows that he expects the saints to know when he says something contrary to the gospel he had originally shown them from scriptures.

Paul had showed them the gospel so clearly that he is now training them to subject him to the particulars of the gospel as he had taught them. They were not to subject the gospel to Paul and bend it to fit whatever Paul says. On the contrary, Paul trained them to subject his preaching to the gospel. Even Paul himself! That is how much Paul magnified the gospel.

Paul taught the saints to not make exceptions. They are to judge all the messages that are taught to them. They were to do this irrespective of who the teacher is.

He said, "though we or an angel from heaven preach any other gospel unto you." He included himself amongst those elders whose message was to be scrutinized by the saints.

Paul was not two-faced. He did not teach the saints to refrain from examining what he said while instructing them to examine what every other minister says.

Discernment is not political. It does not play to the gallery. It is guided by the truth of God's word and not by personalities.

What do I do if the elder is wrong doctrinally?

9. As we said before, so say I now again, If any man preach any other gospel unto you than that ye have received, let him be accursed.
Galatians 1:9

Paul said, "As we said before, so say I now again". The matter at hand is pivotal, so he exempts no one. It is "if any man preach any other gospel".

Observe what he says to do. He said, "let him be accursed". What does Paul mean by "accursed"? Is he training the saints to pronounce curses upon the minister in question? No. we do not curse men. "Let him be accursed" means not to accept such teaching.

Paul told the saints at Galatia to examine his words to know whether to accept what he is teaching or not. He was warning the saints at Galatia against blind followership. The danger of blind followership is that it prevents true growth. Therefore, there is no discernment.

The problem at Galatia is that of elders who left the flock wide open to "grievous wolves" who came in and taught contrary to the gospel. The elders, who had the oversight, should have taken a firm stance against that teaching which had troubled the Galatians.

Paul taught that the saintly response to these false teachers was "let him be accursed". To illustrate his points about dealing with false doctrine, Paul instructs from the Peter-was-to-be-blamed teaching in Galatians 2:1-16.

The application of Paul's Antioch illustration is that there should be elders in Galatia, who, like Paul at Antioch, would ensure that perversion is rebuked and corrected. By teaching all the saints in the churches of Galatia about what had happened at Antioch, Paul was teaching the saints discernment! The elder therefore also trains the saints in discernment.

"Let him be accursed" refers to how discernment works. Have nothing to do with fleshly doctrine or its practice.

Paul's Galatian letter shows that the elder uses sound doctrine to train the minds of the saint, so they can put discernment into words. The saint is wired to accept sound doctrine. A good disciple of Christ, who has been taught the gospel should then recognize if his teachers later "preach any other gospel unto you than that which we have preached unto you.".

Such saints, who recognize that their teachers are now teaching contrary to what they had taught initially, would not be the ones to rebuke or correct these elders. Other elders must correct the elder whose doctrine or practice does not align with the truth. This is Paul's lesson from his rebuke of Peter in the Antioch church.

In all these, the elders are training the heart of the saints in the truth. They are training the saints to recognize honour. It would have been poor example setting for the saints, if Paul had done nothing to correct Peter over the issue in Antioch. It would also have been dishonorable if the saints ignore Paul's oversight and take it upon themselves to rebuke Peter.

There is a healthy tension between discernment and honour. The two are not opposed to one another. There are things that the saint knows are wrong. The saint knows not to receive this into his heart. However, the saint trusts that the elders would do right by God by bringing correction to the assembly.

So, as part of their spiritual growth, the saints have a scriptural responsibility to weigh the actions of the elders and to examine the things that are taught to him or her. The saint is responsible for his or her own heart.

Whereas, the elders over the local assembly have a scriptural responsibility to weigh the actions of the elders and to examine the things that the elders teach to the assembly, they also rebuke other elders as a demonstration of their care and oversight over the flock. The flock learns from this and see this as a demonstration of the elder's care.

Although, the saint would not rebuke the elder, but would trust other elders to do that, the saint should be free to discuss the matters in question with the elders of the local assembly. The saint bringing such matters up for private dialogue with the elder has not done wrong for doing so. Both parties are to have proper dialogue and hear each other out. Both the elder and the saint would do this in a way that shows that both are open to the truth of God's word.

When people are new to this, the tendency is to be disruptive or ill-mannered. The fleshly answer in the face of these possibilities is that many elders discourage or out rightly forbid such engagements. Nevertheless, if this was taught to the saints and modelled for them to see, the saints will get better at engaging the elders in a honorable way.

The saint understands that rebellion is an ever-present danger. Therefore, the saint guards the heart by maintaining a humble heart within the perimeter of God's word. This dialogue can be had without the saint succumbing to the urge to rebuke the elder.

Both the elders and the saints want to have these conversations conscious that biblical discipleship requires ongoing healthy dialogue. Now some cultures and societies are more welcoming of such conversations than others. Sometimes when people feel offended, it is their culture that is kicking in. However, since the gospel encourages healthy dialogue as a practice of discipleship, we subject our cultural biases to the gospel standard.

The elder, who is a disciple of Christ, wants to continue to be able to train the saints as disciples of Christ, while the saint wants to keep his or her heart in a way that allows the saint to continue to receive doctrine from the elder.

Elders that protect the saints

1. And certain men which came down from Judaea taught the brethren, and said, Except ye be circumcised after the manner of Moses, ye cannot be saved. 2. When therefore Paul and Barnabas had no small dissension and disputation with them, they determined that Paul and Barnabas, and certain other of them, should go up to Jerusalem unto the apostles and elders about this question.
Acts 15:1-2

In the local assembly at Antioch, certain teachers came from Judea and taught. Since Paul and Barnabas were the elders at the local assembly at Antioch, they were responsible for what gets said on that pulpit.

The saints would be responsible for their hearts - whether they accepted what was taught or not. Paul and Barnabas would be responsible for cleaning up the mess in the assembly, for they were the elders.

Observe that Paul, Barnabas and the saints listened to these teachers from Judea. We do not know if all the saints discerned that what was being taught was contrary to the word or not. Luke focused on Paul and Barnabas' reaction because that is what determines whether the assembly at Antioch would be wiped out by toxic traditions or not. Luke's emphasis is an investigation of what Paul and Barnabas would do, given that these ministers were from "headquarters".

The chief role of the elders is to train the saints by upholding the word. These Judean elders were not doing so, for what they were teaching was contrary to the gospel.

Now also notice that it was Paul and Barnabas who had no small dissension and disputation with these ministers who they had allowed to preach in Antioch church. Paul, Barnabas, and others in the Antioch church went up to Jerusalem unto the apostles and elders about this question.

The fact that there was "this question" over which Paul, Barnabas and the ministers from Jerusalem disagreed, shows that the local church is not a place for one-way conversation where the teacher instructs all the other people, who sit quietly taking their notes, unable to ask questions.

Paul and Barnabas' disputation and big dissension show that the elder is to ensure that the saints can see them modelling the fact that saints are not to outsource the development of persuasion, conviction and discernment. In their response, Paul and Barnabas were training the saints to use their minds while listening to doctrine. This shows that saints are to examine what is being taught to them.

When Paul, Barnabas and the ministers from Jerusalem were unable to resolve the matter, they did not tell everyone to leave each man to his conviction. They determined to "go up to Jerusalem unto the apostles and elders about this question". They did not say, "let's have a big argument in from of the saints and let them judge who is wrong and who is right". Ministers are best suited for rebuking and correcting ministers.

Who did what?

In Antioch, Pastor Barnabas was not walking in the word, but the saints at Antioch were not the ones who corrected Pastor Barnabas. If they had recognized that Pastor Barnabas was to be blamed, that would have been discernment. If they had rebuked or corrected Pastor Barnabas, there would have been no scriptural basis or example for that. That would have been dishonour. While the saints correcting a minister is be dishonour, those saints knowing that a minister is wrong, is not.

What if Paul had not rebuked the others in Antioch? The saints will not rebuke their Pastor. They have a duty to maintain their discernment.

Elders who do not receive scriptural correction from other ministers show that they cannot be corrected by God's word. Those are not good shepherds but bad examples. Even then, the saint does not assume the role of rebuking or correcting such elders. The saint has a decision on his or her hand whether to stay on in that local church or to move on to a local assembly where evil communications would not corrupt good manners.

Feed the flock

I
t might surprise some that the church is not democratic – it is not governed by a majority-carry-the-vote ideal. It is not merely a case of expressing ourselves, opinions and voices. It is about giving a voice to His word.

15. in case I am delayed, to let you know how people ought to conduct themselves in the household of God, because it is the church of the living God, the support and bulwark of the truth.
1 Timothy 3:15 (NET)

There is behaviour expected of the saints in the local church. This behaviour is taught.

Feed the flock

Peter charged the elders with feeding the flock:

2. Feed the flock of God which is among you, taking the oversight thereof, not by constraint, but willingly; not for filthy lucre, but of a ready mind; 3. Neither as being lords over God's heritage, but being ensamples to the flock.
1 Peter 5:2-3

The assignment of the elders? Feed the flock of God which is among you. The word translated feed, in "Feed the flock of God," is a word that means to shepherd. The expression "Feed the flock of God" is in aorist-imperative. Thus, a do-it-now type of command. It implies urgency.

Thus, the elders know their grave duty of ensuring that the saints are fed. They must not delay this. If the saint is fed with a rich spiritual diet, it would be because the elder has done his job well. Paul repeated the charge to the elders at the Miletus ministers conference:

28. Take heed therefore unto yourselves, and to all the flock, over the which the Holy Ghost hath made you overseers, to feed the church of God, which he hath purchased with his own blood.

Acts 20:28

The flock is the church of God for "he hath purchased with his own blood". These elders are to take oversight by taking heed to themselves and to all the flock. This oversight is in the feeding of the church of God. Paul does not assume that the flock is responsible for locating the food by themselves. He tasks the elders with feeding them. Where is the elder getting this food from?

32. And now, brethren, I commend you to God, and to the word of his grace, which is able to build you up, and to give you an inheritance among all them which are sanctified.

Acts 20:32

On account of the charge that he had given earlier that they were to feed the flock, Paul commended these elders to God by commending them to His word. It is God's word that the elder is to look up to, for building up the elders for the task of exercising oversight.

The gravity and criticality of the office of the elder are amplified by the fact that Paul had sent for the churches by sending for their elders. Once the elders received the charge, it would get to the saints via the elders who feed the assembly the spiritual riches in the word.

The apostolic charge is to the pastors who are to see the word of God as the artillery for taking heed of the flock.

31. Therefore watch, and remember, that by the space of three years I ceased not to warn every one night and day with tears.

Acts 20:31

Paul did not pluck these instructions from thin air, nor did he expect
Paul did not pluck these instructions from thin air, nor did he expect
these elders to figure out how to exercise oversight. He had exercised
oversight over them in his three years of night-and-day training. He
then reminded them that he had warned them all with tears and expected all of them to repeat what they had been rich recipients of.

Eldership is by apprenticeship. Those elders who have been recipients
of the care of an elder are best positioned to faithfully discharge that
duty towards the saints.

Who does the elder feed? The elder feeds the flock of God (see 1
Peter 5:1-2).

Peter, the elder, whose job it is to feed the flock, had said to the flock:

> 2. *As newborn babes, desire the sincere milk of the word, that ye may grow*
> *thereby:*
> *1 Peter 2:2*

The flock is to desire the sincere milk of the word the elders are to
feed them. Where is this sincere milk of the word? The clue to this
that Peter charged the elders to feed the flock. There is a beautiful bal-
ance. Saints desire. Elders feed.

The implication is that the food that the saint needs is not in some
heavenly portal somewhere. It is available wherever the elders are
feeding "the flock of God which is among you". Thus, it is this saint,
who is encouraged to desire the word like the newborn babe, that
Peter tells the elder to feed.

Peter's charge to the saint to desire the sincere milk of the word, is
written to the saint, who Peter expects is being fed the word, by the
elders who feed the flock of God. This is because the flock of God
is with the elders.

> 12. *And we beseech you, brethren, to know them which labour among you, and*

are over you in the Lord, and admonish you; 13. And to esteem them very highly
in love for their work's sake. And be at peace among yourselves.

1 Thessalonians 5:12-13

Paul is not discussing two things when he says "which labour among you, and are over you in the Lord, and admonish you". He speaks of their labour of admonishing the saints in God's word. This he refers to as their work. The saint should highly esteem the elders on account of their work. The saint is to highly esteem the elders on account of their work.

Paul also commands the saints to notice the elders "which labour among you". He shows that their labour is their admonishing.

Therefore, when both Peter and Paul instruct the saints to give the word a higher priority, he has in mind their reception of the ministry of the word given through their elders.

How Paul discipled the elders

1. And it came to pass, that, while Apollos was at Corinth, Paul having passed
through the upper coasts came to Ephesus: and finding certain disciples,
Acts 19:1

This is the record of how Paul had met these elders at Ephesus.

8. And he went into the synagogue, and spake boldly for the space of three
months, disputing and persuading the things concerning the kingdom of God.
9. But when divers were hardened, and believed not, but spake evil of that way
before the multitude, he departed from them, and separated the disciples, disputing
daily in the school of one Tyrannus.
Acts 19:8-9

In order that they might be properly trained, Paul had to separate these disciples so they could receive intense teaching in the word of God as he disputed daily in the school of Tyrannus.

9

Following God

Do not depart from Jerusalem

1. The former treatise have I made, O Theophilus, of all that Jesus began both to do and teach, 2. Until the day in which he was taken up, after that he through the Holy Ghost had given commandments unto the apostles whom he had chosen: 3. To whom also he shewed himself alive after his passion by many infallible proofs, being seen of them forty days, and speaking of the things pertaining to the kingdom of God: 4. And, being assembled together with them, commanded them that they should not depart from Jerusalem, but wait for the promise of the Father, which, saith he, ye have heard of me.
Acts 1:1-4

After His resurrection, Jesus gathered the people together and taught all the apostles as well as many disciples together for 40 days. That was God's plan in action.

While teaching the saints, Jesus gave them commandments. One of such commandments was that they should not depart from Jerusalem but wait for the promise of the Father that He had taught them about. Waiting in Jerusalem was God's plan for the saints as a community. Those who were not fellowshipping with the saints at that time would miss out. All that they were to do was to be gauged in line with Jesus' instruction to that community.

The instruction to wait in Jerusalem was a key leading of God. Since these instructions came while the saints were gathered to listen to Jesus, the practice of gathering together with the other saints is the greatest expression of following the leading of God. This is the single instruction on which the rest of the book of Acts hinges. There is a significant operation of God where the assembly is led as a group in the local church.

This means that when Jesus gathered them together to teach them for 40 days, that gathering was the very will of God. At that time, the saints should have to seriously, prayerfully reconsider having a reason for not heeding Jesus' instruction for them to come together to hear His instructions. Jesus is God's will in action. It is in His instructions to those disciples that each man and woman would find God's will.

Luke records the same instruction:

44. And he said unto them, These are the words which I spake unto you, while I was yet with you, that all things must be fulfilled, which were written in the law of Moses, and in the prophets, and in the psalms, concerning me. 45. Then opened he their understanding, that they might understand the scriptures, 46. And said unto them, Thus it is written, and thus it behoved Christ to suffer, and to rise from the dead the third day: 47. And that repentance and remission of sins should be preached in his name among all nations, beginning at Jerusalem. 48. And ye are witnesses of these things. 49. And, behold, I send the promise of my Father upon you: but tarry ye in the city of Jerusalem, until ye be endued with power from on high.
Luke 24:44-49

Observe that it was as Jesus explained the word to the gathered saints that the instruction was given. The teaching prepared them for the instructions. The direction to "tarry ye in the city of Jerusalem" was spoken to the group. A good way of interpreting the plan of God is to observe the general directions that come to the local church.

It was in this setting that Jesus appointed an elder:

Seeing the will of God

16. He saith to him again the second time, Simon, son of Jonas, lovest thou me? He saith unto him, Yea, Lord; thou knowest that I love thee. He saith unto him, Feed my sheep.
John 21:16

These sheep were the other apostles and disciples of Jesus that were present in the first local church. Peter was to let Jesus express His pastoral abilities through Peter's labour amongst the flock. Jesus' appointment of Peter as a leader to exercise oversight over the whole group was the will of God in action. That was the leading of God for that assembly. Jesus appointed Peter, knowing that His plan in the earth depended on this singular appointment.

Just as the assembly had discerned God's will in Jesus' instructions, the saints would discern God's will in Peter's oversight and the gathering of the local church.

1. And the apostles and brethren that were in Judaea heard that the Gentiles had also received the word of God. 2. And when Peter was come up to Jerusalem, they that were of the circumcision contended with him, 3. Saying, Thou wentest in to men uncircumcised, and didst eat with them. 4. But Peter rehearsed the matter from the beginning, and expounded it by order unto them, saying, 18. When they heard these things, they held their peace, and glorified God, saying, Then hath God also to the Gentiles granted repentance unto life.
Acts 11:1-4,18

The other apostles knew that Peter stayed faithful to Jesus' assignment. They knew that Peter's actions were not to be taken lightly. They grilled Peter because they knew that Peter's actions were important and not to be trivialized.

Peter on his own would know the grave responsibility associated with God's work through him amongst the community of saints. Therefore, he does not take their questions lightly.

They summoned him to have intense discourse because Peter was their elder and, in his actions, they will find the will of Jesus for the church. The apostles and disciples knew that following Peter's godly leadership was following the will of God.

In Peter's eldership, the people that submit to him are in the plan of God. When Peter explained God's leading and dealings with him about the gentiles, Peter, the other apostles and the disciples knew that in understanding Peter, they were understanding God's plan.

James also shows that it was in observing Peter, the elder that Jesus had set over James and the other apostles, that he and the other apostles discerned what God was bringing forth (see Acts 15:14-15).

James could say this because, in Peter's explanation, they concluded that God had granted unto the Gentiles eternal life.

The twelve called the brethren

1. And in those days, when the number of the disciples was multiplied, there arose a murmuring of the Grecians against the Hebrews, because their widows were neglected in the daily ministration. 2. Then the twelve called the multitude of the disciples unto them, and said, It is not reason that we should leave the word of God, and serve tables. 3. Wherefore, brethren, look ye out among you seven men of honest report, full of the Holy Ghost and wisdom, whom we may appoint over this business.
Acts 6:1-3

When there was trouble in the community of saints the elders assembled these disciples in the local church. As Peter spoke to the disciples in response to the troubles in the community of saints, the saints would find God's leading in the words spoken by Peter.

The qualities they were to watch out for were clear. The disciples followed Peter's instruction and in doing so, the will of God was discerned in the church. Likewise, the choice of Stephen, Phillip and the five others was the will of God discerned by the whole assembly of the saints.

Set things in order

5. For this cause left I thee in Crete, that thou shouldest set in order the things that are wanting, and ordain elders in every city, as I had appointed thee:
Titus 1:5

Paul trained Titus to carry out that which Paul would have done, had he remained in Crete. Paul's training of Titus is God's will in action. When Paul left Titus behind in Crete, that was the leading of God. We can see God's leading in Paul's action because it sorted the things that were lacking in the local church. As Titus acted in line with Paul's commands in the local church, Titus was in the will of God. The saints at Crete would be following Christ by following the elders that Titus has ordained in line with Paul's command.

This shows that the saint that follow Paul follow Christ. As those saints follow Titus' scriptural example in the local church, they would be following God. They are in God's will. The saints at Crete would learn the leading of God in learning to follow Titus, who follows Paul.

Discerning God's leading

> *1. Now there were in the church that was at Antioch certain prophets and teachers; as Barnabas, and Simeon that was called Niger, and Lucius of Cyrene, and Manaen, which had been brought up with Herod the tetrarch, and Saul. 2. As they ministered to the Lord, and fasted, the Holy Ghost said, Separate me Barnabas and Saul for the work whereunto I have called them.*
> *Acts 13:1-2*

As saints, we must remember the role of our assembling with others in the local church and our ability to fine-tune our understanding of God's leading. In Acts 13, the men gathered were in a prayer meeting in the local church at Antioch. They prayed together in order to exercise their God-given ability of utterance. When they yielded to this God-given ability of utterance, they spoke out the words of the spirit. it was these words that they spoke to one another that gave focus to their prayer.

Observe that the utterance did not quench the prayer, for spirit-inspired utterance does not quench prayer. The utterance only gave the prayer focus and direction. They were still going to continue to pray together as saints in that local assembly.

Barnabas and Saul who were the elders of that assembly were present. This would have been a meeting convened by them. Thus, it was a meeting of the local church.

It is obvious that this prayer that they prayed together as an assembly was as directed by the spirit of God. What were they praying about? The prayer was about those words, "separate me Barnabas and Saul for the work whereunto I have called them". Thus, they were being led together as an assembly to pray out Paul's and Barnabas' ministry for the years to come.

Since it was to "the work whereunto I have called them," it means that the prayer did not give Barnabas and Saul clarity. Clarity is of the indwelling spirit received in the New Birth. Their prayer, in that prayer meeting, was to commit everyone to the clarity that had already been supplied to Barnabas and Saul.

What was the result? They laid hands on Barnabas and Saul. Thus, in their prayer they had utterance and, in the utterance, they had the spirit's guidance to lay hands upon Barnabas and Saul in separating them to further ministry.

We would be correct to say that the trigger to the ministry of Barnabas and Saul, was that people yielded to give that utterance. It is more correct to say that they got into utterance because they had been praying together as the local church. The Holy Ghost's separation of Barnabas and Saul to the work of God was hidden in their taking out time to gather with the saints in the local church.

Such utterance that reminds people of God's plan and separates people unto ministry tends to come when the saints are gathered in the local church. The will of God is our gathering together and we find God's will in assembling with other saints. In this, we give ourselves opportunities to discerning God's will, His purpose and His plan.

There is such a thing as the plan of God for a meeting. The saints of old knew this. we need to relearn this.

Those that gather in the local church tend to pray together. Those that pray together get into the real intent of that day's assembly. This radically altered the lives of Paul & Barnabas.

The expression "the work whereunto I have called them," means that some things had already been spoken to Paul. Those same things had also been spoken to Barnabas. That makes sense that the spirit had previously told them both, since God had not called "him" but "them". It was obvious to Barnabas that he was to do something with Paul.

> *25. Then departed Barnabas to Tarsus, for to seek Saul:*
> *Acts 11:25*

Barnabas went to Tarsus to look for Saul.

> *26. and when he found him, he brought him to Antioch. So for a whole year*
> *Barnabas and Saul met with the church and taught great numbers of people.*
> *The disciples were called Christians first at Antioch.*
> *Acts 11:26 (NIV)*

Barnabas brought Paul to the church in Antioch and they ministered together to the local church.

> *15. But the Lord said unto him, Go thy way: for he is a chosen vessel unto me,*
> *to bear my name before the Gentiles, and kings, and the children of Israel: 16.*
> *For I will shew him how great things he must suffer for my name's sake.*
> *Acts 9:15-16*

Ananias already knew, by the spirit, that the Lord would use Paul for great things. We do not know whether Ananias knew about Barnabas and Paul forming a ministerial tag-team.

The Holy Ghost said

2. As they ministered to the Lord, and fasted, the Holy Ghost said, Separate me Barnabas and Saul for the work whereunto I have called them.

Acts 13:2

It was in the prayer meeting in the local church that the various things known by each person came together in a clearer picture.

We observe that when the Lord communicates with His saints, He anticipates that those saints that He has spoken to will participate in the local assembly, where He will communicate further through other saints who are gathered in the church. The Lord will speak to others in the local assembly.

3. And when they had fasted and prayed, and laid their hands on them, they sent them away. 4. So they, being sent forth by the Holy Ghost, departed unto Seleucia; and from thence they sailed to Cyprus.

Acts 13:3-4

In the local church, those who gave utterance and those who received it prayed about the utterance together.

Observe that Acts 13:3 says, "they sent them away." The "they" are the other brethren gathered in the meeting with Barnabas and Paul. However, just one verse after Luke had said that it was men that had sent Barnabas and Paul forth, Acts 13:4 says, "they, being sent forth by the Holy Ghost".

Luke wants us to see that the activity of the Holy Ghost is the activity of those men who had gathered with Barnabas and Paul in the local church at Antioch. The action of the local church is taken to be the mind of the Lord. Thus, Barnabas and Paul found their path in God's plan as they stayed in the local church.

This shows that the local church is a way of establishing God's will on a matter and that the saint is wired to thrive in God's will, as we stay in the local church. Therefore, saints commit self-harm when they think that they need time away from the local church in order to find themselves.

The Holy Ghost witnesses

22. And now, behold, I go bound in the spirit unto Jerusalem, not knowing the things that shall befall me there: 23. Save that the Holy Ghost witnesseth in every city, saying that bonds and afflictions abide me.
Acts 20:22-23

Observe that term the "Holy Ghost witnesseth". What is the Holy Ghost witnessing to? The "Holy Ghost witnesseth" to the leading that Paul already had – he said, "I go bound in the spirit unto Jerusalem". Just as in Acts 13:3-4, where "being sent forth by the Holy Ghost" refers to the saints in the assemblies speaking out utterance, here the "Holy Ghost witnesseth" through those saints speaking out utterance in every city where Paul had gone to.

Where would this witnessing have taken place? In the local church through the saints.

Since the "Holy Ghost witnesseth" in every city, it means this witnessing is irrespective of the city. When saints gather in fellowship, the leading of the Holy Ghost is amplified.

The leading of the spirit in the local church goes together with the leading of the saint. The leading of the spirit is two-fold: what you know within and what is uttered by those that you assemble within the local church. These two should not be separated.

When Barnabas went looking for Saul so Paul could partner in the ministry committed to Barnabas by Peter and the other elders, Barnabas was in the will of God, Paul's willingness to partner with Barnabas was the leading of God in action. That leading was clearly discernable in Paul's response to Barnabas.

The well-taught saint fine-tunes the meaning given to God's leading in the local church. to abandon the local church is not beneficial to the saint. When Barnabas, Paul and the three other ministers met together in Antioch, that was the will of God. The leading of God was discernable in the things these ministers spoke to one another in that meeting, which was a special ministers' meeting in the local church.

Command and Teach

37. If any man think himself to be a prophet, or spiritual, let him acknowledge that the things that I write unto you are the commandments of the Lord.

1 Corinthians 14:37

Paul affirmed that the mature disciple would recognize that the things that Paul had written to the Corinthians were "the commandments of the Lord."

Let no man therefore despise him

10. Now if Timotheus come, see that he may be with you without fear: for he worketh the work of the Lord, as I also do. 11. Let no man therefore despise him: but conduct him forth in peace, that he may come unto me: for I look for him with the brethren.

1 Corinthians 16:10-11

Paul's testimony about Timothy is noteworthy. The saints at Corinth are to recognize that despite his youthfulness, Timothy "worketh the work of the Lord, as I also do". It is on account of this that Paul tells the church at Corinth "let no man therefore despise him". Since, according to Paul, Timothy taught what Paul taught, there was no legitimate grounds for the saints to despise Timothy.

Today, when the elder of the local church commands the people to do what Paul and the apostles commanded in scripture, the saints and the elders are to know that those things that the elder commands are the commandments of the Lord. If, however, the elder abandons the teaching of the apostles, the saints would have grounds for despising such a minister.

Let no man despise thy youth

Here's what Paul told Timothy:

> *12. Let no man despise thy youth; but be thou an example of the believers, in word, in conversation, in charity, in spirit, in faith, in purity.*
> *1 Timothy 4:12*

We can learn from what is not said as much as we can from what is said.

The Greek word translated "despise" in "Let no man despise thy youth" is the word kataphroneo. "Kata" means down, while Phren is mind, therefore phroneo is to think. So, this word literally means think down upon and by implication to despise because it is thought to be without value. It means to "think little of".

The expression "Let no man despise" is in the present imperative. It is stated with a prohibition. Thus, Paul is forbidding an action that is already happening from continuing.

Observe that Paul did not say, "Let no man despise thy youth; but if they do, give them a public warning". Rather, he said, "Let no man despise thy youth; but be thou an example...". This means that the God-given way to not let anyone despise your youth is by not failing in your God-given power of setting a solid example for the saints.

The "let no man despise thy youth" was up to Timothy. Amongst other things, he would have done this by being an example in his doctrine. If an elder is not an example of sound doctrine, and the saints despise him or her as a result, the elder is responsible for turning that around by commanding what the apostles commanded and not violating their commands himself.

The Greek word translated "example" in "but be thou an example of the believers" is a word that means an example to be imitated, or the pattern to be followed. Paul used this same word in admonishing Titus:

> 7. *In all things shewing thyself a pattern of good works: in doctrine shewing uncorruptness, gravity, sincerity, 8. Sound speech, that cannot be condemned; that he that is of the contrary part may be ashamed, having no evil thing to say of you.*
> *Titus 2:7-8*

It is the word that has been translated "example" that has been translated "pattern" in "shewing thyself a pattern of good works." The elder is to show the good work of being incorruptible in doctrine. The elder has also been commanded to exercise oversight by feeding the flock of God the word of God. This is a sacred task with eternal consequences.

Command and teach

> 28. *And it came to pass, when Jesus had ended these sayings, the people were astonished at his doctrine: 29. For he taught them as one having authority, and not as the scribes.*
> *Matthew 7:28-29*

The people were astonished at Jesus' doctrine because He taught with authority. Christ is our example in the conduct of ministry and in the giving of the word to our hearers. Based on this example the apostles give commands about how the word is to be taught effectively.

> 6. *If thou put the brethren in remembrance of these things, thou shalt be a good minister of Jesus Christ, nourished up in the words of faith and of good doctrine, whereunto thou hast attained. 7. But refuse profane and old wives' fables, and exercise thyself rather unto godliness. 8. For bodily exercise profiteth little: but godliness is profitable unto all things, having promise of the life that*

now is, and of that which is to come. 9. This is a faithful saying and worthy of all acceptation. 10. For therefore we both labour and suffer reproach, because we trust in the living God, who is the Saviour of all men, specially of those that believe. 11. These things command and teach.

1 Timothy 4:6-11

Observe how Paul instructed Timothy to minister - command and teach.

Here are other renderings of the eleventh verse:

Prescribe and teach these things.
1 Timothy 4:11 (NASB)

In the footnote of the NASB, we find an alternate rendering "Keep commanding and teaching."

The Amplified renders it this way:

Keep commanding and teaching these things.
1 Timothy 4:11 (AMP)

The Greek word translated "teach" means to provide instruction in a formal or informal setting with the highest possible development of the pupil as the goal. We are explaining in such a way that the will of the student becomes conformed to the teaching taught.

The Greek word translated "command" was used in medicine to describe the doctor's prescription or instruction to the patient. The patient was bound to follow the doctor's instructions if he wanted to get well! The word means to announce something that must be done. We give words to be obeyed.

Paul tells Timothy the verb form four times in 1 Timothy – 1 Timothy 1:3; 5:7; 6:13,17. He told Timothy the noun form twice in 1 Timothy – 1 Timothy 1:5,18.

Interestingly, both the Greek words translated "command" and "teach" are in the present imperative. It means it is habitual. You never arrive. The pastor does not do this once in a while but continuously. The present imperative verb refers to a process. It is a setting in which you can never say, "I've arrived!" Which means that Timothy is to continue to command and teach.

Command and teach are Timothy's ongoing patterns.

What is Timothy to command and teach? Paul said, "these things". Whenever we see expressions like "these things", we pause and ask "What things?" in this passage, it'll be those things that Paul had commanded in verses 6 to 10. Timothy was to command those things that Paul had just taught him about. The commands of Paul were to be regularly prescribed and taught to those under Timothy.

Observe that Paul did not just want Timothy to give knowledge about godliness. Timothy's oversight meant that he was expected to command and teach these things. He was to teach with authority and boldness because he was saying the commands of the Lord, which He had conveyed through Paul.

Paul tells Timothy the following:

12. Let no man despise thy youth; but be thou an example of the believers, in word, in conversation, in charity, in spirit, in faith, in purity.
1 Timothy 4:12

"Let no man despise thy youth" implies "do not act your age". It is spoken to the pastor and not the saints that he or she has just been told to command and teach. It is not up to the saints. It is up to the pastor who will not act his or her age but instead acts the revelation knowledge that God had given the apostles. The elder is to know that he or she works the work of the Lord as Paul did.

Timothy was to give himself to sound doctrine and show his maturity in his conduct for the believers to see. Timothy was therefore to be an example of the believers. He was to use sound doctrine and its conduct to motivate the saints and cause their hearts to open to him.

Then the people would see that the messenger giving the command is exemplary in conduct.

Why would Paul say this after telling Timothy to habitually command and teach the saints?

It is because people find it hard to respect a do-as-I-say-and-not-as-I-do person. It is hypocrisy to say one thing and do another. When actions do not match words, there is an integrity problem. People who lack integrity, lose credibility. We do not trust or respect the do-as-I-say-and-not-as-I-do person.

Although God's word is the reality of the highest order, if its teachers lack integrity, they will lose credibility, and people will not take God's word seriously. Yet, the message is the very power of God! Therefore, the elder who has presented a perfect Saviour to the saints in words is now told to present Him in the conduct of a sound doctrine.

13. Hold fast the form of sound words, which thou hast heard of me, in faith and love which is in Christ Jesus.
2 Timothy 1:13

This is in the present imperative, therefore it is a command. Timothy is aware that Paul is commanding him.

Timothy had heard the form or outline of pure doctrine from Paul. Paul had mapped out the territory and Timothy has it in his possessions. Timothy was to prize it as that which a man should not lose. To "hold fast" means that he was to keep pure doctrine in his possession always.

Timothy is not to look for something new because if that new thing had been beneficial, the apostles would have taught it. Paul had been very thorough in training Timothy. The implication is that it is the old heresies that the Lord and His apostles already dealt with that get dressed in new clothes. The answers given by the apostles are all that we need.

The idea is that if you hold fast to the word, the power of the written word will strip your mind of the tendency to abandon the old-and-true while going after the new-and-fanciful. We can say of your mind, "truth lives here."

2. And the things that thou hast heard of me among many witnesses, the same commit thou to faithful men, who shall be able to teach others also.
2 Timothy 2:2

You have heard me teach many things that have been confirmed by many reliable witnesses. Teach these great truths to trustworthy people who are able to pass them on to others.
2 Timothy 2:2 (NLT)

Paul's "among many witnesses" means publicly. These are not things spoken in secret but in the open.

What Timothy has heard will determine how he reasons and this will be the guide of his actions.

What Paul passed to Timothy, Timothy was to pass to faithful men and the faithful men are to pass it on to others. Timothy commits to other faithful men, the same doctrine he has learnt from Paul.

16. Take heed unto thyself, and unto the doctrine; continue in them: for in doing this thou shalt both save thyself, and them that hear thee.
1 Timothy 4:16

If Timothy, and the men he has trained take heed to continue in the doctrine of the apostles, he would save himself and his hearers from error and the development of practices that are contrary to that of the apostles.

The elder best saves those that hear him by ensuring that he or she commands what Paul and the apostles had already commanded.

Charge some

> *3. As I besought thee to abide still at Ephesus, when I went into Macedonia, that thou mightest charge some that they teach no other doctrine,*
> *1 Timothy 1:3*

That expression "charge some" means that the pastor is to command. The elder commands those teaching in the local church to "teach no other doctrine". There are many things that people try to pass off as doctrine. The pastor is to know the doctrine of the apostles and then continually charge that no other doctrine be preached. Doctrine is that critical.

This means that Timothy himself taught no other doctrine but that of the apostles. A pastor can and should command the saints not to teach any other doctrine but that of the apostles. When the pastor is confident that he is speaking the commands of the apostles, he must speak them as commands. In the same way that the apostles did.

The things we command you

> *4. And we have confidence in the Lord touching you, that ye both do and will do the things which we command you.*
> *2 Thessalonians 3:4*

Paul's confidence in the Lord was that the saints would do "the things which we command you."

Observe that Paul speaks of "the things which we command you." This is because Paul who had taught them about the grace of God had given them lots of commandments. Paul's understanding of the revelation of God's grace included giving godly commands so the saints could practice the doctrine.

Note that Paul's command on the outside and God's steer on the inside of the saint agree (see 2 Thessalonians 3:5). Following God does not oppose abiding by scriptural commands spoken by our elders in the local church.

Paul had said:

> *2. For ye know what commandments we gave you by the Lord Jesus.*
> *1 Thessalonians 4:2*

"For ye know" – he is reminding them of the previous teaching.

He had given them those things that the Lord commanded. Since it is by the Lord, Paul is saying that the things that the saints are to do those things that he has commanded. When we say what Paul says, those things are to be done.

> *11. And that ye study to be quiet, and to do your own business, and to work with your own hands, as we commanded you;*
> *1 Thessalonians 4:11*

> *This should be your ambition: to live a quiet life, minding your own business and working with your hands, just as we commanded you before*
> *1 Thessalonians 4:11 (NLT)*

> *That you make it your ambition to be living a quiet life, that you are cultivating the habit of attending to your own private affairs, and that you are working with your hands, even as I gave you a charge,*
> *1 Thessalonians 4:11 (WUEST)*

He also commanded them to work with their hands. Living by this command was to be their ambition!

That word "that you study" is from a Greek word that means "from a love of honour to strive to bring something to pass", "to strive earnestly, make it one's aim." It denotes restless eagerness in any pursuit, hence, "to strive eagerly, to be zealous." Paul is describing how the disciple should respond to these commands.

They had been overly excited, abandoning responsible living because the thought the Lord was coming the next minute. Now he commands them to pour that energy into abiding by the command to live in the word.

There is a false idea that the more disconnected a saint is from everyday life, the more spiritual he or she is. Really, the Christian walk is seen in everything we do.

10. For even when we were with you, this we commanded you, that if any would not work, neither should he eat.
2 Thessalonians 3:10

He repeats a command he had given "when we were with you." The command was "if any would not work, neither should he eat."

6. Now we command you, brethren, in the name of our Lord Jesus Christ, that ye withdraw yourselves from every brother that walketh disorderly, and not after the tradition which he received of us.
2 Thessalonians 3:6

Although it is not politically correct to say so, the scriptures show that it is the practice of Paul to command the saints.

Again, he commands them "in the name of our Lord Jesus Christ." This means by the authority of Jesus Christ. Thus, there is gravity in his commands. He was not making these things up in order to keep the saints on their toes.

The tense of "we command" is present. This means it is ongoing. It is not a command in the past. Even as he wrote, that command was in force.

He gave instructions about how the saints were to respond to those who disobeyed these apostolic commands. The saints were to withdraw themselves from those saints that disobeyed the traditions which he received of us.

Paul said there were brethren "who walketh disorderly, and not after the tradition which he received of us". He called these commands "traditions" because they were orally passed before these truths were put into written form.

Observe how Paul responded to those that disobeyed the commands. He did not take it personally. He gave further instructions to those that would obey.

It is noteworthy that Paul wanted the saints to see that he had been a wonderful example of the command that he was asking them to obey (see 2 Thessalonians 3:7).

12. Now them that are such we command and exhort by our Lord Jesus Christ, that with quietness they work, and eat their own bread.
2 Thessalonians 3:12

Notice that Paul said, "we command and exhort by our Lord Jesus Christ." Who are the "we" giving the command?

1. Paul, and Silvanus, and Timotheus, unto the church of the Thessalonians in God our Father and the Lord Jesus Christ:
2 Thessalonians 1:1

The epistle was from Paul, Silvanus, and Timotheus to the church of the Thessalonians. Thus, Paul, Silvanus, and Timotheus were the "we" that were commanding the Thessalonians.

Again, we observe that Paul had commanded and exhorted by our Lord Jesus Christ, which means his commands were by the authority of Jesus Christ.

Paul's disposition towards the saints was "we have confidence in the Lord touching you, that ye both do and will do the things which we command you" (see 2 Thessalonians 3:4). It is the same confidence that Timothy was to have when he commanded the people to do what Paul had instructed in the scriptures.

11. Prescribe and teach these things.
1 Timothy 4:11 (NASB)

Note that Timothy knew to command what Paul had commanded in his epistles, which are teachings. Paul actually told Timothy to teach and to command or prescribe. This means that we see to it that we explain what people are to do from the word of God. We clarify. We instruct. The saints are to have their obedience birthed in clarity. Paul's instructions to Timothy to command the saints is within the setting of Timothy teaching those commands already contained in scripture. Timothy is standing on the shoulder of the apostles.

Teaching explains the truth. Commanding is the mode in which you do it. Command and teach go together. This means the pastor diligently studies the scriptures to be sure the meaning of the text is clear. The pastor sees what the Lord wants to be done in His commands which have been given by the apostles, then the pastor stands to teach the assembly. He or she must not explain the truth as if we were communicating suggestions. The heart of those who hear the teaching must be very clear that what is said is obligatory, for they are the words of God because they are the words of His apostles.

The saints are to anticipate that in conducting their ministry in the local church, the elders will command the saints. If those commands agree with the word, the saints are to see those commands as the commandments of the Lord, which must be obeyed by the saints. The elder teaches knowing that the lives of the disciples who are gospel-soldiers are at stake. Their wellbeing depends on the training and insight of their elder.

Command them that are rich

17. Charge them that are rich in this world, that they be not highminded, nor trust in uncertain riches, but in the living God, who giveth us richly all things to enjoy; 18. That they do good, that they be rich in good works, ready to distribute, willing to communicate;
1 Timothy 6:17-18

"Charge them" means to command them. Paul commands Timothy

to command those who are rich. Being materially rich does not give any special advantage to the rich saint in the local church. a man's wealth does not exempt him from the command of the elder. It is a sad situation if the pastor cannot command those saints that are rich.

High-minded refers to Paul's earlier warning when he instructed Timothy about "corrupt minds, and destitute of the truth, supposing that gain is godliness." This is a reference to covetousness. Paul's instructions show that in Timothy's scriptural charge, those rich saints who were also covetous would find recovery.

The saints' response

12. And we beseech you, brethren, to know them which labour among you, and are over you in the Lord, and admonish you; 13. And to esteem them very highly in love for their work's sake. And be at peace among yourselves.
1 Thessalonians 5:12-13

13. Think highly of them and give them your wholehearted love because of their work. And remember to live peaceably with each other.
1 Thessalonians 5:13 (NLT)

Interestingly, Paul's "we beseech you" is from a Greek word which means to plead, implore, to beg. While he is authoritative, he is not coming across as authoritarian. He reminds all that they are brethren. Therefore, he is talking to brethren who need to tackle the problem in the local assembly at Thessalonica regarding what he is about to discuss.

The saints are to recognize the worth of those elders who are among them. They should not take the elders for granted. These are "them which labour among you".

"Among you" means in the local church.

The expression "are over" in "are over you in the Lord" could mean either to preside, lead, direct or to protect, give aid, give attention to and to care for.

The phrase, "them which ... are over you in the Lord," is a tricky translation.

How many people readily see that the expression means "know them which labour among you, and give aid to, give attention to and care for you in the Lord"?

"In the Lord" means that Paul was not discussing secular leaders.

We recall Paul was addressing brethren. Christianity is a brotherhood. So, Paul was not teaching who is "under" versus who is "over". He was teaching the high estimation and recognition of those brethren whose labor among you by standing in front to lead the whole group. Paul is instructing these saints to follow their leaders.

Whereas the saint can be blessed by other ministers that uphold sound doctrine, there is a special treatment that the saint must give to the elders which labour "among you". These are the elders that command and instruct the saints.

The scriptures assume that the elder that commands and instructs you is someone you see face to face. There is a relationship. Others might teach us, but it is our pastors that command, instruct, caution or warn us.

The saints hold these elders in the highest regard in love. The highest regard is for the elder in the local church. We think of them very highly (over, beyond and above highly) and lovingly on account of our recognition of their labour. Paul exaggerated this point for emphasis. All this is on account of their work, else their work might not benefit us.

The Greek word that has been translated "over you" in "over you in the Lord" is a word that means to be placed before, or first, to lead. The word means "to have an interest in", "caring for", "being enthusiastic about", and so on. The idea is that the elder is one who cares for the people and has an interest in them.

This means that the elders support people in love and care for them. Their commands and charges are ways of expressing their care for the flock. When the saints resist or ignore sound, godly commands, there will be no "peace among yourselves",

The saints are to esteem the elders very highly, warm up to and look forward to receiving their commands and so their work would bring forth godly fruit in the saints. The saints are to love these elders. This esteeming of our elders very highly means that the default posture of the saint is "I will obey these commands" and not "why should I obey them? who do they think that they are?".

When elders command what the apostles have commanded in the word of God, the elders are not to be despised. We might not like the command because it is not comfortable, but it is for our good. The heart that resists the godly commands of the elders doubts the integrity of God's word. It leads to loss of peace in the local church.

Do not lord it over

2. Feed the flock of God which is among you, taking the oversight thereof, not by constraint, but willingly; not for filthy lucre, but of a ready mind; 3. Neither as being lords over God's heritage, but being ensamples to the flock.
1 Peter 5:2-3

As an under-shepherd of God's flock, the elder does not lord it over the flock. Peter commands the elder, who is to command the saints, not to lord it over the saints.

However, the oversight of godly, strong, healthy elders who confront spiritual lethargy, firmly confront open sin, or challenge the saints to walk in the word, might be wrongly labelled lording it over the saints. That would be an incorrect conclusion.

Despite this, the elder is to command obedience to the word. If an elder makes a judgment call, which goes against your opinion, without demeaning or devaluing you, that is not lording it over or abuse.

The elder that discredits others, or condemns them or shames them while trying to make them walk in the word would be lording it over. However, godly oversight can be strong without lording it over.

11. Now no chastening for the present seemeth to be joyous, but grievous: nevertheless afterward it yieldeth the peaceable fruit of righteousness unto them which are exercised thereby.
Hebrews 12:11

A significant portion of God's chastening would come via the local church.

Generally, it is as people yield to correction and rebuke that their growth becomes evident. While being rebuked, people do not find it palatable.

11

Observe these things

15. And in those days Peter stood up in the midst of the disciples, and said, (the number of names together were about an hundred and twenty,) 16. Men and brethren, this scripture must needs have been fulfilled, which the Holy Ghost by the mouth of David spake before concerning Judas, which was guide to them that took Jesus. 17. For he was numbered with us, and had obtained part of this ministry. 18. Now this man purchased a field with the reward of iniquity; and falling headlong, he burst asunder in the midst, and all his bowels gushed out. 19. And it was known unto all the dwellers at Jerusalem; insomuch as that field is called in their proper tongue, Aceldama, that is to say, The field of blood. 20. For it is written in the book of Psalms, Let his habitation be desolate, and let no man dwell therein: and his bishoprick let another take. 21. Wherefore of these men which have companied with us all the time that the Lord Jesus went in and out among us, 22. Beginning from the baptism of John, unto that same day that he was taken up from us, must one be ordained to be a witness with us of his resurrection. 23. And they appointed two, Joseph called Barsabas, who was surnamed Justus, and Matthias. 24. And they prayed, and said, Thou, Lord, which knowest the hearts of all men, shew whether of these two thou hast chosen, 25. That he may take part of this ministry and apostleship, from which Judas by transgression fell, that he might go to his own place. 26. And they gave forth their lots; and the lot fell upon Matthias; and he was numbered with the eleven apostles.
Acts 1:15-26

Luke shows how the one hundred and twenty assembled disciples recognized that there was to be the twelfth apostle who was to replace Judas. They knew to pray.

By their prayer and selection process they partnered with the Lord in doing His work on the earth amongst men and practiced how to discern the leading of God as a group.

In other to do this, Peter had to stand up. Peter based his steer on a solid grasp of scriptures. People who are given to the word, who want to flow with God's leading as a group, know that the scriptural way to arrive at that clarity is by cooperating with those elders in whose actions they discern the leading of the spirit.

Peter gave the qualities that must be met. This is what the spirit was doing in the community of saints. Peter was following the word. The word has instructions about the vacant apostleship. We see that Peter's oversight is to emphasize those things that the word provides teaching on.

This is what elders are. They see to it that the saints act on the written word. When the leader acts on the word, what the elder is instructing at that point in time is what the spirit wants to be done at that time.

Observe that none of the others gets up to say he or she has been shown differently. That would be unwise and fleshly. Peter was acting on and was guided by the word.

It is noteworthy that we do not have a similar account of Peter standing up to have the saints choose which saints should marry one another.

Peter was this prescriptive because the ministry of Matthias was not a personal thing but the discerning of God's will for the whole assembly. It required the elders.

On the other hand, the spouse that a saint marries is to be an act of personal consecration and devotion. It is not a decision the whole church makes for the saint. It is not even a choice the pastor makes for you.

18. And all things are of God, who hath reconciled us to himself by Jesus Christ, and hath given to us the ministry of reconciliation; 19. To wit, that God was in Christ, reconciling the world unto himself, not imputing their trespasses unto them; and hath committed unto us the word of reconciliation.

2 *Corinthians 5:18-19*

Each saint should act on the ministry of reconciliation by preaching the gospel. The elders train the saints how to do this in the assembly. The assembly should heed the scriptures that command us to preach the gospel. The elders call the assembly to act on this as one.

The elders are to teach the saints the clear message of the gospel and ensure that the saints understand its content. The elders can assemble the saints so the saints, as a group, can act on the word of reconciliation together.

In Acts 2, they were having a prayer meeting that quickly turned into an outreach meeting. As Peter got up to preach to everyone, the other eleven apostles directly supported him.

The other saints got everyone present to listen to Peter's sermon, which was what the spirit of the Lord was doing at that time. Peter was expressing it.

The elder upholds and is an enforcer of those things commanded in the written word. Since the content of the ministry of reconciliation, which has been given to each saint is in the written word, the elder is to train the saints in its expression.

However, the elder would have done a shoddy job if the saints are unable to preach the gospel when the only way they can preach the gospel is that which is organized by the local church.

Consider that, while the local church is out evangelizing together, the indwelling spirit might independently prompt the saints who are out preaching together to pay attention to different individuals to who they should minister. It is not the whole assembly that should stop to minister to that person. The pastor has done a good job when the saints know that what the spirit is doing at that point is through that saint as he or she responds to God's leading and ministers to the one hearing the gospel.

The saints will have a life outside of the local church. As they go about their everyday life, opportunities to preach the gospel will emerge. The saints must be free to take those opportunities without feeling guilt that it was not done in the local church.

There is no tension of personal evangelism versus the local church evangelizing together. When the local church is reaching out in evangelism, that would not be the time to claim emergency leading that prevents participation in the church's since you are led to do your own. The saint that refers to the spirit as the reason for not participating in the assembly is in pride. Such habits would be despising the church and its leaders.

The elders that command the saints to preach only when together with the other saints are also injuring the saints.

The Lord who works with the assembly is the indwelling Spirit instructing each saint.

Apostles' feet

36. And Joses, who by the apostles was surnamed Barnabas, (which is, being interpreted, The son of consolation,) a Levite, and of the country of Cyprus,
37. Having land, sold it, and brought the money, and laid it at the apostles' feet.
Acts 4:36-37

Luke's observation that Barnabas "laid it at the apostles' feet" means that the saints practised giving as taught by the apostles. A saint who is properly taught in the word would be seen practising giving as taught by the apostles because that is the teaching of the word.

Here's Paul's instruction to Corinth:

1. Now concerning the collection for the saints, as I have given order to the churches of Galatia, even so do ye. 2. Upon the first day of the week let every one of you lay by him in store, as God hath prospered him, that there be no gatherings when I come. 3. And when I come, whomsoever ye shall approve by your letters, them will I send to bring your liberality unto Jerusalem. 4. And if it be meet that I go also, they shall go with me.
1 Corinthians 16:1-4

Paul said, "as I have given order to the churches of Galatia, even so do ye." Thus, what he said was to be their practice. We see that Paul taught the Galatians and Corinthians to give. His teaching was in detail.

Giving as prospered is the apostolic principle. Once the saint gives as prospered, the pastor's labour has paid off. The job is done.

We do not despise the word

If the elder in Corinth got up and demanded that each saint must give a specific amount, that elder would be supplying oversight beyond the ability of God's word. In addition, such an elder is disobedient to Paul's order, which he has given the churches. Making a specific amount compulsory and referring to that as the leading of God is not what the spirit had said to them through Paul. The pastor that enforces such despises Paul, the local assembly and the Lord. That is a sin to be repented of. Such an elder is in the same boat as the saint that claims he was led to apply pressure tactics on the saints. They would all be contradicting the Lord, who had given Paul what to tell the assembly of saints in the local church.

18. And when Simon saw that through laying on of the apostles' hands the Holy Ghost was given, he offered them money, 19. Saying, Give me also this power, that on whomsoever I lay hands, he may receive the Holy Ghost. 20. But Peter said unto him, Thy money perish with thee, because thou hast thought that the gift of God may be purchased with money. 21. Thou hast neither part nor lot in this matter: for thy heart is not right in the sight of God. 22. Repent therefore of this thy wickedness, and pray God, if perhaps the thought of thine heart may be forgiven thee. 23. For I perceive that thou art in the gall of bitterness, and in the bond of iniquity.

Acts 8:18-23

Peter's response to Simon's offer of money is instructive. He responded that was because he knew that Simon's heart was "not right in the sight of God". Thus, Simon was not being led by the spirit of God. There was a way to give in the apostles' doctrine. Simon's words were the practice of the world, showing that he despised Peter. If did not he would have given according to the apostles' doctrine. Peter knew what the written word commanded and as an elder, he upheld the written word.

We do not despise scriptural elders

11. But when Peter was come to Antioch, I withstood him to the face, because he was to be blamed. 12. For before that certain came from James, he did eat with the Gentiles: but when they were come, he withdrew and separated himself, fearing them which were of the circumcision. 13. And the other Jews dissembled likewise with him; insomuch that Barnabas also was carried away with their dissimulation. 14. But when I saw that they walked not uprightly according to the truth of the gospel, I said unto Peter before them all, If thou, being a Jew, livest after the manner of Gentiles, and not as do the Jews, why compellest thou the Gentiles to live as do the Jews?

Galatians 2:11-14

Peter's action influenced Barnabas and others. Paul showed that Peter's action amid those saints deviated from the truth of the gospel. Peter knew the truth of the gospel but did not uphold it. He abandoned his God-given oversight.

Although Peter was acting amid the assembled saints and was a noted pillar amongst them, the saints ought to have discerned that Peter had rebelled against the word, on account of good training already received via the apostles. Saints who are following Peter in such a scenario are despising the word.

It is not a teaching of the scriptures to teach the saints to blindly follow the pastor. Even in such cases, an elder would get up to provide the direction for the assembly. This is what Paul did in Antioch.

Paul knew the truth of the gospel. Although the others have not upheld the word, Paul was going to uphold its teaching so that the saints could receive proper training as disciples. This means Paul did not abandon oversight.

On the other hand, if while in the Antioch assembly what Peter had done did not deviate from the word, the saints would have done well to follow his godly example, for he gave oversight. When scriptural oversight is given but ignored, we despise the word.

We do not despise the assembled saints

3. Wherefore, brethren, look ye out among you seven men of honest report, full of the Holy Ghost and wisdom, whom we may appoint over this business. 4. But we will give ourselves continually to prayer, and to the ministry of the word. 5. And the saying pleased the whole multitude: and they chose Stephen, a man full of faith and of the Holy Ghost, and Philip, and Prochorus, and Nicanor, and Timon, and Parmenas, and Nicolas a proselyte of Antioch:
Acts 6:3-5

The Lord had given direction to the saints via the elders, who had given themselves to the word. These elders then gave instructions to the saints that they had trained in the word.

These assembled saints functioned as a single unit when assembled. There is to be no division. The leading for that entity called "the assembly" is the elders, who themselves are people of the word, prayer and the ministry of the word. Since the oversight of the assembly is given to the elders, this would not be apart from the elders, who have been commanded by God to feed the flock.

The instructions of the elders would be the direction for the assembly. The saint who separates himself from the assembly saying the spirit has told him how to identify the leaders is confused and divisive.

1. Now Peter and John went up together into the temple at the hour of prayer, being the ninth hour.
Acts 3:1

The church had "the hour of prayer". It was a time that the saints assembled and prayed together. Peter and John were keeping with this tradition.

13. And when they were come in, they went up into an upper room, where abode both Peter, and James, and John, and Andrew, Philip, and Thomas, Bartholomew, and Matthew, James the son of Alphaeus, and Simon Zelotes, and Judas the brother of James. 14. These all continued with one accord in prayer and supplication, with the women, and Mary the mother of Jesus, and with his brethren.
Acts 1:13-14

The upper room was their lodging. All these saints gave themselves to continuing "with one accord in prayer and supplication,". So, there are times the saints assemble in order to prayer extensively.

24. And when they heard that, they lifted up their voice to God with one accord, and said, Lord, thou art God, which hast made heaven, and earth, and the sea, and all that in them is: 31. And when they had prayed, the place was shaken where they were assembled together; and they were all filled with the Holy Ghost, and they spake the word of God with boldness.
Acts 4:24,31

The saints were gathered at a prayer meeting, in unity. The assembly waited to hear Peter and John's report. It was not just a random scenario where some prayed while Peter and John informed the saints. No one groaned in prayer when the time came for Peter and John to provide instruction.

There are various types of meetings in the assembly. One of those meetings is one where the saints gather to pray. This is the prayer meeting. Such times of prayer are not accidental. As it is a meeting of the assembly, oversight is needed which would be provided by the elders.

The pastor should teach about prayer in order that the saints know how to conduct themselves during these times of prayer. The saints respond by coming for the prayer meeting and by giving themselves to prayer. The saints would know how to and how not to pray given that the elders would have given excellent teaching on what not to pray about from the emphasis of the scriptures.

In response, the well-taught saints pray.

Then, "they lifted up their voice to God with one accord" means that the elders led the saints in prayer and the assembly joined the elders in prayer because it was scriptural.

Prayer is the will of God. That is beautiful and of God. It was not random. It is the product of continuing in the apostles' teaching.

It would be weird for one of the saints to withdraw from that time of prayer because the "spirit" had told that saint that the assembly should be doing something else. The Lord can get through to Peter and John!

While the elders are the ones to assemble the saints, and while it is true that they are the ones that supply the teaching regarding prayer to the saints, it is the indwelling spirit and not the elder that would bring supernatural knowing, illumination and other experiences in prayer.

It is the spirit that reveals things to the saints in prayer or would have them focus their prayer as the assembly prays. The assembly might be praying for the saints and as they pray there may be one or two who are impressed upon to pray for specific saints. That is a detail that the pastor is not responsible for. The pastor is not the indwelling spirit, who dictates whether the saint should pray or not pray.

To each, his sphere

3. But Peter said, Ananias, why hath Satan filled thine heart to lie to the Holy Ghost, and to keep back part of the price of the land? 4. Whiles it remained, was it not thine own? and after it was sold, was it not in thine own power? why hast thou conceived this thing in thine heart? thou hast not lied unto men, but unto God.

Acts 5:3-4

Observe Peter's words to Ananias: unsold the land remained Ananias'; after the land was sold, it was Ananias' own. Peter let Ananias know the demarcation between what was in Ananias' power and what was not.

There is a sphere that the elders are not responsible for. This is the area dealing with the personal space of the individual not the local assembly. It is not the saints gathered as the entity called "the assembly."

The pastor is responsible for things in the local church.

In the personal space

39. The wife is bound by the law as long as her husband liveth; but if her husband be dead, she is at liberty to be married to whom she will; only in the Lord.

1 Corinthians 7:39

Paul's command from the Lord is that there is no command on the specific saint that another saint should marry. The saint is at liberty to be married to whom she (or he) will only in the Lord.

Paul is the one teaching this God-given power of choice to the saints. the elder's oversight would be that of ensuring the saints know not to go marry an unbeliever or to be unequally yoked.

The elder's oversight might involve letting the saints know that they should not just marry a person because they are born again. There are saints that do not bring out the best in each other. This is however easier if the saint asks the pastor to get involved as the saint makes these choices. The pastor should teach the saints not to be unequally yoked but to make godly choices.

The pastor would not be exercising oversight if he or she now acts as the enthroned judge who determines who marries and who does not marry amongst the saints on account of his clout and influence. That would be lording it over the saints.

One of the great functions of the elders is to train the saints to recognize the difference between godly oversight and being lorded over in the private sphere of life. When these choices are exercised in private life, the pastor would not make the saints feel that the pastor is responsible for such choices. That only leads to abuse.

He rebuked the saints together

6. Your glorying is not good. Know ye not that a little leaven leaveneth the whole lump? 7. Purge out therefore the old leaven, that ye may be a new lump, as ye are unleavened. For even Christ our passover is sacrificed for us:
1 Corinthians 5:6-7

Paul was speaking of the power of influence when he said, "know ye not that a little leaven leaveneth the whole lump?". When dealing with this brother he addressed the whole church.

9. For to this end also did I write, that I might know the proof of you, whether ye be obedient in all things.
2 Corinthians 2:9

Paul addressed the saints in Corinth as if they were all in the same boat. He used their reaction to his epistle to know "whether ye be obedient in all things", notwithstanding the fact that not all of them went about with their father's wives.

17. Now in this that I declare unto you I praise you not, that ye come together

not for the better, but for the worse.
1 Corinthians 11:17

"Ye come together" refers to the whole assembly. Paul observed them as an assembly. He said, "in this that I declare unto you I praise you not." He could not praise them as an assembly because they gathered for the worse. He did not say "but one of you does not." The whole assembly was judged together.

5. I speak to your shame. Is it so, that there is not a wise man among you? no, not one that shall be able to judge between his brethren?
1 Corinthians 6:5

Again, Paul addressed the whole assembly and said, "I speak to your shame". He said, "Is it so, that there is not a wise man among you". He did not spare them. He said, "no, not one". He observed them as an assembly and found them wanting. Since was true of the assembly was true of each, then the whole assembly was judged together and rebuked together.

1. O you dear idiots of Galatia, who saw Jesus Christ the crucified so plainly, who has been casting a spell over you?
Galatians 3:1 (PHILLIPS)

Paul referred to the whole assembly as "dear idiots of Galatia". He considered all as being under a spell because of the power of influence.

So we see that when Paul rebuked the Corinthians and Galatians, he rebuked the collective. What we learn from the fact that the whole church got rebuked is that scripturally speaking, the local assembly that a saint abides reflects the true slant of their heart.

20. how I wish I could be with you now and change my tone, because I am perplexed about you!
Galatians 4:20 (NIV)

Paul addressed the whole assembly and said "I am perplexed about you". Any saint in Galatia who insisted that Paul's assessment was wrong and who saw himself as an exception would have been deluded. The saint the church in Galatia shared in the rot of others and needed to heed the apostolic rebuke. You are where you fellowship.

It is rather sobering that every time local churches were rebuked by the apostles, in the bible, the whole assembly was rebuked together. Your local church might be a stronger commentary about you than you are willing to admit. It is an uncomfortable fact that our local church tells us a lot about ourselves and not just about the local church itself.

5. Remember therefore from whence thou art fallen, and repent, and do the first works; or else I will come unto thee quickly, and will remove thy candlestick out of his place, except thou repent.
Revelation 2:5

The Lord told the saints in Ephesus to repent. The whole assembly.

17. Because thou sayest, I am rich, and increased with goods, and have need of nothing; and knowest not that thou art wretched, and miserable, and poor, and blind, and naked: 18. I counsel thee to buy of me gold tried in the fire, that thou mayest be rich; and white raiment, that thou mayest be clothed, and that the shame of thy nakedness do not appear; and anoint thine eyes with eyesalve, that thou mayest see. 19. As many as I love, I rebuke and chasten: be zealous therefore, and repent.
Revelation 3:17-19

The Lord's assessment was at the local church level. "Thou sayest, I am rich, and increased with goods" is a reference to their doctrinal slant towards materialism. While you could say not everyone was deficient you cannot reach that conclusion by reading John's letter.

He told that whole assembly, "thou art wretched, and miserable, and poor, and blind, and naked:"

The Lord's rebuke through John's ministry in the book of revelation shows us that it is impossible to separate a man from the local assembly that he is a part of.

We should observe these things.

Praying smartly

31. And the Lord said, Simon, Simon, behold, Satan hath desired to have you, that he may sift you as wheat: 32. But I have prayed for thee, that thy faith fail not: and when thou art converted, strengthen thy brethren.
Luke 22:31-32

Satan asked to sift Peter because Peter was pivotal to the church of the Lord Jesus, which would come into being from the resurrection of Jesus. Satan understood the gravity of Peter's role.

Peter was not the only one that had a post-resurrection ministry. However, Peter was a significant trigger whose influence could neutralize most of the others. This is an uncomfortable fact.

Jesus did not dismiss the threat to Peter. Jesus' understanding of the gravity of Peter's role caused Him to pray for Peter. When Jesus prayed for Peter, He was showing us that that was the most effective way to pray for all the others. So, we pray well for the whole assembly when we spend time praying for our pastors.

18. Pray for us: for we trust we have a good conscience, in all things willing to live honestly.
Hebrews 13:18

The elder who wrote the book of Hebrews gives a grave command - Pray for us.

When the pastors live honestly, the saints that are affected by their example are also motivated to live honestly. Thus, praying for the elders of the local church is not praying for one man or woman. There is a ripple effect through time.

1. Finally, brethren, pray for us, that the word of the Lord may have free course,

and be glorified, even as it is with you: 2. And that we may be delivered from
unreasonable and wicked men: for all men have not faith.
2 Thessalonians 3:1-2

There are wicked and unreasonable men who bring danger to Paul and the elders. Paul did not say, "Don't worry. It is nothing. Think nothing of it". He said, "Finally, brethren, pray for us"

The Lord's men are pivotal to His plan on the earth via His operation through these men and women in the local churches. Their loss is a loss for a myriad of men. This is why we pray for our elders.

Consider Herod who went after Peter:

1. Now about that time Herod the king stretched forth his hands to vex certain
of the church. 2. And he killed James the brother of John with the sword. 3.
And because he saw it pleased the Jews, he proceeded further to take Peter also.
(Then were the days of unleavened bread.) 4. And when he had apprehended
him, he put him in prison, and delivered him to four quaternions of soldiers
to keep him; intending after Easter to bring him forth to the people. 5. Peter
therefore was kept in prison: but prayer was made without ceasing of the church
unto God for him.
Acts 6:1-4

Peter's life was in danger. In response, "prayer was made without ceasing of the church unto God for him". Peter was someone the saints needed to pray for. There are consequences when we neglect to do so. Imagine if Peter had died before the Acts 15 meeting?

In your prayer life, praying for your pastor is the most efficient way to ensure that you will stay in the will of God. It takes the elders, for the local church to assemble. Therefore, in the absence of the elders, we do not have a local assembly, though we might have saints. Therefore, the best way to preserve the local assembly is to pray for your elders.

When we pray for our pastors, we pray for our local assemblies and its saints.

A Theatre for questions and answers

We are to go into all nations, preaching in His name.

His feet. Their feet.

> *14. How then shall they call on him in whom they have not believed? and how shall they believe in him of whom they have not heard? and how shall they hear without a preacher? 15. And how shall they preach, except they be sent? as it is written, How beautiful are the feet of them that preach the gospel of peace, and bring glad tidings of good things!*
> *Romans 10:14-15*

The gospel is powerful but of itself it does not save men until preachers take its message and proclaim it to other men. So, the preacher is important.

"How shall they hear without a preacher".

Paul was teaching from Isaiah:

> *7. How beautiful upon the mountains are the feet of him that bringeth good tidings, that publisheth peace; that bringeth good tidings of good, that publisheth*

salvation; that saith unto Zion, Thy God reigneth!
Isaiah 52:7

Isaiah speaks of "the feet of him that bringeth good tidings". That "Him" is Jesus. Thus, Jesus is the gospel preacher that publishes salvation.

In Paul's teaching, he doesn't speak of "him" but of "them".

This means that Isaiah's "his feet" is Paul's "their feet". This shows that the saints are the hands and feet of Jesus in carrying His gospel everywhere. He is giving His service to men through our words and our slant. In other words, Jesus carries out His proclamation by us. Whenever we preach, we are to represent His message properly.

The feet of "Him" is the feet of "them" because as His body, we are identified with Him in His mission to men. This is in order that men might know what the Lord has done.

Preach repentance

Observe what Jesus said:

45. Then opened he their understanding, that they might understand the scriptures, 46. And said unto them, Thus it is written, and thus it behoved Christ to suffer, and to rise from the dead the third day: 47. And that repentance and remission of sins should be preached in his name among all nations, beginning at Jerusalem.
Luke 24:45-47

After explaining the scriptures to His disciples, he sent them to preach "his name among all nations, beginning at Jerusalem".

How were they to preach? They were to preach the way they had seen Him preach. He opened "their understanding, that they might understand the scriptures". That means He opened their minds to understand the message by bringing its many parts together to form a whole.

The intent was that "repentance and remission of sins should be preached in his name".

Their preaching was for repentance. Thus, the aim of preaching is in order that men might change their minds. In this case, it was a change of mind with respect to how God remitted sins.

Our ministry, just like that of the disciples is with repentance in mind. This means that the men that we are speaking to have the wrong mentality about God's action. In order to change their minds, we bring them "a new mind" as our gift to them when we preach in His name.

We bring the mind of God to the mind of men in order that men might swap their thoughts for God's thoughts given through His word properly explained.

This means that we preach to men because they have a mind. If men did not have a mind, there would be no need for preaching. Implied in the act of preaching is the admission that the men we are teaching are not zombies. We want their minds engaged because God wants their minds engaged.

The gospel content is not ours. It is God's. The approach is also God's. we are not looking for mysterious things to drop into the spirits of men. our task is to engage the minds of men.

Jesus opened their understanding by speaking until they abandoned their former mindset and received His, which He presented in His explanations of scriptures. We are not trying to get to the spirits of men but to their minds. He spreads through us the fragrance of His knowledge.

Forty days of infallible proof

To whom also he shewed himself alive after his passion by many infallible proofs,

being seen of them forty days, and speaking of the things pertaining to the
kingdom of God:
Acts 1:3

As we read this, we recall that the writer of the book of Luke is also
the writer of the book of Acts, where more detail about the Luke 24
episode is given.

From Luke 24, which covers the same time frame, we see that the
"many infallible proofs" that Jesus gave for forty days were His explanation of writings of Moses, the prophets and the Psalms.

Whereas reading Luke 24, it might appear that the expounding happened in a few minutes, Luke shows in the book of Acts 1 that the
teaching was over 40 days. Jesus gave them 40 days of proof. He produced the proof from the holy scriptures, which He explained to open
their understanding.

This is sobering indeed. It took Jesus forty days of extensive teaching
after the resurrection, to convince people that had been around Him
for three and a half years before the cross.

Jesus brought His disciples to repentance by His patient, extensive
presentation of the truth. We will also bring men to repentance by our
patient, extensive presentation of the truth to those men. This is the
hardness that the teachers of the word are to endure as we preach to
men in the local assembly.

We preach the Jesus message the Jesus way. We keep bringing men
extensive proofs from the scriptures because each man has a mind
and people need different depth and volume of proof from scriptures
because their minds had been plugged into wrong slants.

The mind of the world

17. This I say therefore, and testify in the Lord, that ye henceforth walk not as
other Gentiles walk, in the vanity of their mind,
Ephesians 4:17

The problem of men is the walk in the vanity of their mind. This walk is a mind thing. An understanding that is called "the vanity of their mind". It is referred to as vanity because they would not accept the knowledge of Jesus. Their thought process is vain because it has not received the gospel.

The men who walk in the vanity of their minds are those unbelievers who have not received the logic of God into their minds. Paul's admonition is that the saint must not think like one who has not received gospel-light. It is on account of this vanity of the mind that the understanding needs to be opened.

How did Jesus do it?

3. To whom also he shewed himself alive after his passion by many infallible proofs, being seen of them forty days, and speaking of the things pertaining to the kingdom of God:
Acts 1:3

Jesus opened the minds of His disciples by showing them "many infallible proofs". Thus, in His practice, we see His command for us to preach to men by giving them many infallible proofs from scriptures. Jesus preached that way for 40 days!

Men and their questions

6. When they therefore were come together, they asked of him, saying, Lord, wilt thou at this time restore again the kingdom to Israel?
Acts 1:6

Interestingly, after 40 days of astonishing insight through Jesus' teaching, the people who had heard Him asked, "wilt thou at this time restore again the kingdom to Israel?". He had been teaching them about the kingdom of God (see Acts 1:3), yet the men that had been listening to Him for 40 days were still thinking about the kingdom of Israel!

Jesus answered the question of His disciples.

> *7. And he said unto them, It is not for you to know the times or the seasons, which the Father hath put in his own power. 8. But ye shall receive power, after that the Holy Ghost is come upon you: and ye shall be witnesses unto me both in Jerusalem, and in all Judaea, and in Samaria, and unto the uttermost part of the earth.*
> *Acts 1:7-8*

He answered their question. What was the answer? - "And he said unto them, it is not for you to know".

In other words, although they were asking Him about the kingdom of Israel, that wasn't what He was giving them.

The text reads better if we mentally took "And he said unto them, it is not for you to know" and we mentally place it at the end of verse 6 instead of at the start of verse 7. That way, we put His answer together with their question. In which case, He is saying "I did not promise you that which you are asking about"

We easily forget that the book of Acts is a letter.

The verses that we have in our English Bibles were put there by Europeans. Originally, of all the books of the bible, only the book of Psalms had chapters. This changed when an English man, Stephen Langton, added the chapters while teaching in Paris. About 300 years later, a French printer-scholar Robert Estienne introduced verses to the chapters.

Seen this way, Acts 1:7 would start with "to know the times or seasons which the father has put in his power ... but ye shall receive power, after that the Holy Ghost is come upon you...".

Jesus is saying that you will do all you are to do by the spirit. While He did not promise the kingdom of Israel, He promised that they would take the spirit and do things by the spirit.

While Jesus was teaching them for forty days, they were thinking the kingdom was Israel when it was the spirit. they had a blocker in their minds.

Jesus, the great shepherd, was One that His students could approach with questions.

Notice that He had preached, He had opened their understanding, He had given infallible proof, and yet their questions reflected that they still needed to clarify their understanding.

This "wilt thou at this time restore again the kingdom to Israel?" is a mind-numbing question, which doesn't come across as sensible.

Did Jesus ignore their questions? No. Jesus answered. When these men asked their questions, Jesus answered. This is how Jesus trained those men that turned the world around. Jesus let them talk.

A man does not lose his brain because he has heard the gospel, because he is in church or because he is listening to the clearest of teachers.

Peter, who shook the world at Pentecost, was a question-asking-disciple. All the disciples were students that had questions when they were taught. They got better with clarification. From there they got up and changed their world.

It is noteworthy that Jesus was not an unquestionable teacher. Therefore, when we carry His message to men, we carry the content and that manner of His, which allowed men to have and ask questions until clarity was birthed in their minds.

The example that we see as we observe Jesus the great shepherd of the sheep is that He anticipated questions which he allowed the men to ask. If it appears like He is unquestionable today, it is because we, who are His hands and feet, that proclaim His message, are unquestionable.

The example we see in Jesus, after His three years teaching pre-cross and forty days teaching post-resurrection, is that no matter how detailed we are, and how accurate we are, the men that listen to us will have questions

People questioned Jesus before the cross

9. Who hath ears to hear, let him hear.10. And the disciples came, and said unto him, Why speakest thou unto them in parables?
Matthew 13:9-10

"Who has ears to hear, let him hear" means "if you give attention in faith, you will get understanding".

His disciples questioned His approach saying, "Why speakest thou unto them in parables?". These disciples who questioned Him barely understood His teaching. Yet, in verse 11, "He answered and said unto them". Jesus was explaining the teaching of Moses, the prophets and the psalms (see Luke 24:44).

Combining what we see of Jesus in Matthew pre-resurrection and what we see in Acts post-resurrection, we have a glimpse of what our local assemblies must be like if we are to produce the disciples that will doggedly cover the earth with the gospel.

If after the teaching of Jesus, the One that all Israel called the Rabbi, the people needed to ask further questions, it is understandable and expected that after ours, people might still have many questions.

Thus, we see that Jesus' teaching and His teaching slant is instructive.

We must raise men like Jesus raised disciples. Our style is found in His.

The Acts 1 passage shows that whatever power Jesus received post-resurrection, it wasn't a power to forbid men from asking Him questions.

As His disciples, we observe His method too. We teach with authoritative clarity while anticipating that our disciples in the local churches would have questions.

The gospel is a dialogue

2. And Paul, as his manner was, went in unto them, and three sabbath days reasoned with them out of the scriptures, 3. Opening and alleging, that Christ must needs have suffered, and risen again from the dead; and that this Jesus, whom I preach unto you, is Christ.
Acts 17:2-3

Observe the manner of Paul. He reasoned from the scriptures. He was opening and alleging, which was how he produced infallible roofs from scripture. His message was Christ. If the teacher is reasoning out of the scriptures, his students will also reason along.

Again:

8. And he went into the synagogue, and spake boldly for the space of three months, disputing and persuading the things concerning the kingdom of God. 9. But when divers were hardened, and believed not, but spake evil of that way before the multitude, he departed from them, and separated the disciples, disputing daily in the school of one Tyrannus. 10. And this continued by the space of two years; so that all they which dwelt in Asia heard the word of the Lord Jesus, both Jews and Greeks.
Acts 19:8-10

Notice that Paul preached by "disputing and persuading the things concerning the kingdom of God" for three months!

Can you dispute all by yourself? He was responding to men in order to persuade them. This shows that in order to properly disciple men the gospel must be presented as a dialog.

Observe that prior to the separation, he had been disputing for three months and that after the separation, he was still disputing. He was disputing because he appealed to the minds of men. Whenever men start thinking, questions start coming forth.

Consider the example of Jesus:

18. Absolute deity in its essence no one has ever yet seen. God uniquely-begotten, He who is in the bosom of the Father, that One fully explained deity.
John 1:18 (WUEST)

The word translated "explained" in "fully explained deity" is a word that means "to declare by making plain", "tell the meaning of something, especially to tell it fully", "to make known", "clear by providing more detail", or "thoroughly explain". Jesus brings out the meaning of God. Jesus is the detailed and systematic explanation of the character of God. This is the origin of the English word exegesis. Exegesis interprets a text, based solely on what it says. It says what is in the text as opposed to reading into it what is not there (eisegesis). Jesus is the proper exegesis of God. In Him, we see what God is saying about Himself as well as what He is not saying. Jesus is the authoritative bringing forth into visibility of that which was there all the time about God, but which was not seen until brought forth.

Jesus is God's explanation of Himself in ways that our mind can grasp. Jesus is the intimate secrets of God. When He speaks of God, He speaks about Himself. Jesus is the explanation or exegesis of the Father. What we want to see about God, we observe in Jesus.

46. And it came to pass, that after three days they found him in the temple, sitting in the midst of the doctors, both hearing them, and asking them questions.
47. And all that heard him were astonished at his understanding and answers.
Luke 2:46-47

Where was Jesus? He was in the Temple among the doctors. What was He doing? He was listening to the doctors, who were the experts in the writings of Moses, the prophets and the Psalms. Jesus was both hearing and asking them questions. What is God like? He will be found in the temple amongst men. What was He not doing? He was not participating in the rituals and sacrifices.

His presence in the temple is instructive. Although we find Him in the temple, He is with those discussing and explaining the scriptures and not with those slaughtering the animals for the rituals!

Thus, the temple was designed for education. It was to be the school of learning Moses and the prophets. It was to be the house of opening the understanding of men through preaching and teaching so that men could understand the purpose and plan of God in redemption. It was not to be a house of rituals and other human traditions.

How are we this sure? We trace God's will in the actions of Jesus. God's proof was in what He did when He came to the temple.

He showed that the temple was not the issue, it was what people did in it that required clarification. He did not come to the temple for the ritual of the heave offering, a burnt offering, or other ritualistic sacrifices but for teaching, questions and answers in dialogue with knowledgeable men.

God proved that He will be found listening to teachers. More importantly, He will be found asking those teachers questions after listening to them.

This is the same Jerusalem Temple that others had assumed was the home of animal sacrifices, all manner of offerings and other forms of ritualistic worship. Jesus did not go to the temple to offer or receive ritualistic sacrifices or to show the best way to kill those various animals.

He went to the temple to receive learning and to sharpen His understanding. The temple had always been a place for study, discipleship, teaching, questions, contributions, and answers.

God is the kind of student who hears you well and asks you questions after hearing you. He will not rush. However, He will ask questions. God is at home among men that did not despise Him being a student or on account of His age. This is the Father explained.

46. And it came to pass, that after three days they found him in the temple,

sitting in the midst of the doctors, both hearing them, and asking them questions.
47. And all that heard him were astonished at his understanding and answers.
Luke 2:46-47

What kind of student is Jesus? He expects His teacher to anticipate that He would understand and that He will have answers as well as questions. He won't have just one or the other but both.

Thus, we see that people can have questions and answers at the same time. Jesus was the student in that temple-setting. The doctors were the teachers. The Lord validates that there is a way to engage the Lord.

The people that heard Jesus were astonished. While listening and asking, He built and expressed a formidable and accurate understanding.

In listening to those teachers, He became a better teacher than them. This is to be expected. His questions were not a hindrance but a help to the raising of disciples of Christ. Questions show that men are thinking.

We were not told that Jesus had been listening to any other sets of teachers asides from those ones in that temple and yet while listening to them, questions arose.

When God shows up in our local assemblies, what would He expect to see? He will expect to see teaching, listening, questions, answers and dialogue.

We observe that it was in Jesus asking questions and watching good men answer questions, that He developed that phenomenal ability for answering questions that we later see in His ministry about 18 years later as a 30-year-old. This is the kind of setting that produces teachers like Jesus. If our local assemblies are set up this way, we will raise disciples with stronger convictions.

I concede that in that type of setting there will not be perfect orderliness. However, it will produce the kind of healthy vigorous dialogue associated with education.

What if people's contributions are weird? At the very least, the elder would be able to identify areas where further explanation is needed. Moreover, a weird contribution does not mean that learning is not taking place. We often need to unlearn in order to learn very well.

Jesus encouraged dialogue in His teaching ministry.

What if people abuse the opportunity given to ask questions and to propose answers? It could happen. We also recognize that we are dealing with men on the journey to maturity and who might not have been in that kind of religious setting where the disciples and the elders are in dialogue before.

The response to the possibility of abuse is not to ban or discourage people from asking questions in a teaching setting. The truth is that with time, by and large, the saints get better at being less disruptive, at framing questions well and in presenting their answers knowing the answers will be scrutinized.

We are satisfied that as a student, God in Christ, asked questions.

Jesus' participation in this learning setting, is God's endorsement of the fact that an environment where the bible is being taught should be one where men don't feel they'll be penalized for having questions or asking them.

Jesus the One that asked people questions was very welcoming of people asking Him questions. We should structure our local assemblies to be theaters of dialogue about the gospel.

We are His kind.

Last words

24. And let us consider one another to provoke unto love and to good works: 25. Not forsaking the assembling of ourselves together, as the manner of some is; but exhorting one another: and so much the more, as ye see the day approaching.
Hebrews 10:24-25

First, observe an indisputable fact concerning the saint. The saint is indwelt by God. He or she does not need a place to meet God or to pay our dues to God.

Secondly, observe what the local church is not about. The local church is not our coming into God's presence. Where God's presence is concerned, we permanently have the presence of God in the New Birth.

Thirdly, observe what the local church is really about. The local church is about saints coming into a presence – into each other's presence. We come together as a practice of consecration which is born of the truth of the indwelling spirit. We do not come to meet God but with the indwelling of God's spirit to fellowship with other saints who also have the indwelling of God's spirit.

We assemble as the practice of not forsaking others with whom we understand what it means to be disciples of Christ.

The disciples of Christ come together face to face in order to provoke each other unto love and to good works. Thus, we minister to others and are ministered to.

In the written word, we find God's description of our true characteristics in Him. He says we should not forsake the assembling of ourselves together because His spirit within us wants to get together in face to face meetings with other saints.

In the local church, we separate the saints from un-seriousness.

In the local church, the elders serve by feeding the saints who see themselves as ministers. The key relationships are based on service received and given in the power of God. The local church is a network of ministers who pray, study and nurture young disciples together.

12. Even so ye, forasmuch as ye are zealous of spiritual gifts, seek that ye may excel to the edifying of the church.
1 Corinthians 14:12

The local church is the place to be zealous of spiritual gifts. We want people to be zealous from the consciousness of the ability of the spirit who indwells each saint.

In the local assembly, there are those who are unlearned as well as those who are learned. Both the learned and the unlearned have the same spirit but not the same zeal.

We do not ignore the unlearned in our fellowship meetings. The learned know they are to bear the burden of carrying the unlearned along.

Although we train the saints to carry the unlearned along, we must be careful not to take this to mean that we operate our meetings for the benefit of the unlearned.

Are we dumbing things down to the level of the unserious?

26. How is it then, brethren? when ye come together, every one of you hath a psalm, hath a doctrine, hath a tongue, hath a revelation, hath an interpretation. Let all things be done unto edifying.
1 Corinthians 14:26

We know Paul's setting is the local church because he is describing "when ye come together". He isn't referring to personal life. He speaks of coming together.

Since God commands that all the things we do in the local church are to be done unto edifying, the local church is designed with edification in mind.

We ensure things are structured to emphasize service.

There are no members of the church of Jesus that are without the spirit. By the indwelling of the spirit of God, each member has something to give. So, you are not a spectator in a stadium. Rather, you aim to excel in edifying others. You observe others who yield to the spirit. As you observe others who are serving, you take their yielding as a reminder to respond to the same spirit within you. You are ready to contribute. You are observing the best time to come forward.

You and I see ourselves as expressions of the risen Lord, vessels through which He continues to deliver His service in the local church.

Here is to strong churches that will fill the earth in the last days!

OTHER BOOKS BY AUTHOR

All books available on Amazon

Contact Author

sekou@sekou.me

OTHER BOOKS BY AUTHOR

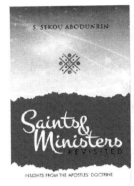

All books available on Amazon
Contact Author
sekou@sekou.me